Corporate BS

*Surviving, Thriving and
Inspiring in the Cubicle Jungle*

By A.D. Napier

ISBN: 978-1-7352129-0-6 (eBook)

ISBN: 978-1-7352129-1-3 (Softcover)

For information regarding bulk purchases of this book, digital purchase and special discounts, please contact

Publisher: Gotham Global Media,
New York
www.GothamGlobalMedia.com

Please continue the conversation at
www.CorpBull.com

Contents

INTRODUCTION
Stranger than Fiction... 1

BACKGROUND
We're Not in Kansas Anymore..................................... 5

CHAPTER 1
The Most Important Lesson.......................................11

CHAPTER 2
It All Starts at the Top..25

CHAPTER 3
You Want the Truth? You Can't Handle the
Truth!..33

CHAPTER 4
Characters in the Corporate Screenplay..............41

CHAPTER 5
The Inmates are Running the Asylum....................47

CHAPTER 6
Every Peg has Its Hole...59

CHAPTER 7
Playing Nice in the Sandbox.....................................69

CHAPTER 8
If You Can't Stand the Heat, Get Out of the
Position...73

CHAPTER 9
You Seem Somewhat Familiar; Have I Threatened You Before?......................77

CHAPTER 10
The Worst Part of the Job............................87

CHAPTER 11
When Mr. Right is All Wrong.....................95

CHAPTER 12
From Great to BS...Another One Bites The Dust..101

CHAPTER 13
The Best Part of the Job.............................113

CHAPTER 14
Badges? We Don't Need No Stinkin' Badges!..119

CHAPTER 15
You Get What You Give...............................125

CHAPTER 16
What We Have Here is a Failure to Communicate..131

CHAPTER 17
Houston, We Have a Problem.................139

CHAPTER 18
Your Get Up and Go has Got Up and Gone........145

CHAPTER 19
Don't Stop Believing..................................149

That's a Wrap!....................................155

"Neurologists say that our brains are programmed much more for stories than for abstract ideas. Tales with a little drama are remembered far longer than any slide crammed with analytics."
John P. Kotter, professor

INTRODUCTION
Stranger than Fiction

From the earliest time I can remember, whenever I experienced something interesting, I immediately started the process of writing about it in my mind. Most times I used these observations as a basis to weave a tale of fiction. Who knew that my actual life in the corporate world would turn out to be more interesting than any of my imaginary stories?

I entered the business world in the mid-1980s when I was hired right out of school by a world-renowned defense contractor as a computer programmer. Ten months later, I was approached by a friend of a friend with the opportunity to become an independent consultant. So I quit my first real job, freaked out my mother, and increased my salary. This started a 25-year journey as both a consultant and an employee that led to Wall Street, banking, retail, the travel industry, health care systems, and then to complex electronics supply chain distribution. I went from being an individual contributor to managing teams with hundreds of people and leading the integration of multi-billion-dollar acquisitions.

During my career I've encountered many challenging situations and many people (both inspiring and aggravating) that often had me thinking, "I should write a book!" So I finally did. However this book is not intended to proclaim some new groundbreaking business theory or transformational idea…it's not a textbook. Instead it's a compilation of my most interesting, thought-provoking, and even comical adventures in the corporate jungle with lessons learned along the way. Some may seem hard to believe, but I assure you that they're all true. So I hope you'll sit back and chuckle at the anecdotes while finding a few points that resonate with your own career. Maybe you'll even be able to avoid some of my mistakes!

I've purposely designed this book to contain chapters that are short and impactful; I'm not looking to waste your time with elaborate theories and irrelevant BS. But don't let the size fool you; bigger is not always better!

For those of you who may be new to the corporate world, on the following pages when I write "C-level" or simply the letter "C," I'm describing someone at the highest level of an organization whose title begins with "C," for example Chief Executive Officer (CEO), Chief Financial Officer (CFO), etc. You get the idea.

While the stories are all true, the actual names of individuals and companies involved have been omitted; instead titles and business sectors are noted. That's because this volume is not meant to be a hit piece. As for the catchy title, please don't get the wrong idea. My intention is not to condemn all companies; there are many great ones that have management who value their employees…and I've had the honor of being employed by some of them! My goal is not to paint every business with one broad brush. But unfortunately even within these outstanding companies there are often plenty of pockets of Corporate BS!

BACKGROUND
We're Not in Kansas Anymore

As a child growing up on Long Island in a lower middle-class family headed by a single parent, I remember taking one of those high school aptitude tests whose results suggested that I should pursue a career as a gym teacher or a blue-collar worker. And to tell you the truth, I was (and still am) perfectly fine with that evaluation. But that's not how things turned out.

Never one to put limits on myself I took my blue-collar expectations into the white-collar world of corporate America. But based on my humble background, I was concerned that I wouldn't succeed in this environment. This lack of confidence made me keenly aware of my surroundings. A shy and quiet kid, I spent much of my early career listening intently, infrequently speaking up, and learning everything I could as quickly as possible.

As my career progressed from an unobtrusive behind-the-scenes contributor to international meetings, corporate jets and expense accounts, my lingering insecurity led me to work extremely hard to feel worthy of this unexpected success.

It didn't take long for me to find massive absurdities in the business world. That's when I began to truly appreciate Scott Adams, the brilliant creator of the Dilbert cartoons. His funny sketches prompted me to start formulating my own views on Corporate BS.

Since a corporation's culture, i.e., its values and principles, are created and institutionalized by its management, BS starts at the top, trickles down, and pervades every level of employment. See what you think of my satirical, yet often true, list of BS characteristics:

You know you're working for BS management if:

- Instead of working productively, more time is spent in useless meetings that have no meaningful outcome

- "Process" has taken the place of human intelligence

- Management spends more time formulating mission statements than writing business plans

- Sales goals and budgets are set from the top down, not bottom up

- Telling the truth and doing the right thing is not a priority

- Actors, Parrots and Chameleons permeate the organization (more on this later)

- The senior executives are more familiar with the bartender at the golf course than the office manager at the local sales office

- Failures and mistakes are not considered learning opportunities, but nails in your coffin

- Technology drives the business rather than the business driving technology

- The Human Resources department operates as a leadership organization, not a support organization

- Reducing staff is considered an accomplishment, not a necessary evil

- The sales force spends more time planning than selling

You know you're working for BS management if:
continued

- The C in the corner office has had his wallpaper or office furniture changed more than once for no good reason

- Managers are criticized for knowing too many details and are told to operate at a higher level

- People are being promoted for the wrong reasons

- No one keeps score

- The organization is made up of insecure people

- Titles are more important than accomplishments

- Assignments are given without the responsibility or resources to make them successful

- Political maneuvering is considered the most important skill for survival

- Organization charts are so convoluted that you can't tell who you report to

Hopefully by now you're nodding in agreement with at least a few of these observations. Each BS characteristic will be addressed as we move through the book.

However in spite of all the BS, the corporate environment can provide you with opportunities beyond your wildest dreams. As you read through this book, please know that I believe working in this world is a privilege. Give it your all and make sure you're earning your paycheck. When you have a bad day, think about all the people who don't have jobs where they are afforded the luxury of working in climate-controlled offices, with indoor bathrooms, while sitting at desks with phones and computers. Nevertheless, we need to be appreciative, but not beholden.

So in **corporate speak**, let's ___open the kimono___ and ___examine core competencies___ so I can hopefully gain your ___buy-in___ as we begin to ___peel back the onion___ and ___grab some low hanging fruit___ in an attempt to ___move the needle forward___ as we ___kick around some ideas___ before ___circling back___ and ___running it up the flagpole___ so ___at the end of the day,___ ___when push comes to shove___, we are not only ___on the same page,___ but on the ___bleeding edge___ because of our ___outside-the-box views___ on the ___paradigm shift___ within today's Corporate world.

Or how about this: We eliminate the BS and discuss what really happens in the corporate jungle using a language we all understand. Follow me and let's have some fun!

"The biggest mistake that you can make is to believe that you are working for somebody else... The driving force of a career must come from the individual. Remember: Jobs are owned by the company; you own your career!"
Earl Nightingale, author

CHAPTER 1
The Most Important Lesson

Here's the most important lesson I learned in my 25-plus-year corporate career: a critical part of your current job must be making sure that you're prepared for your next one. Let me tell you a few stories…

As mentioned in the introduction, my first job was for a top-tier defense contractor. After working extremely hard to learn the intricate code in the computer programs that drove the engineering systems, a coworker told me that her friend had just established an Information Technology (IT) consulting company and was looking for employees who would work as job shoppers, i.e., as someone who would be paid hourly, with no benefits, and typically for a short time frame.

Perfectly happy in my current position, I didn't really consider changing jobs until she explained that I would have the opportunity to work in all kinds of diversified industries, while learning new state-of-the-art technologies. Now I was intrigued. Then when she mentioned the salary, I was sold – it was three times the amount I was currently making! But the downside was that the position could only be guaranteed for four months. The upside was that in those four months, I would make almost as much money as a year's salary at my present job.

Even though it would have been easy to stay in my current position, I wondered if I should push myself to expand my horizons. After some deliberation, I decided that it was a no-brainer and I bet on the chance that the contract would be extended. When I told my mother that I was leaving the big, secure company for a ten-person start-up with an uncertain future, she thought I was nuts!

I remember being nervous when I walked into my supervisor's office to hand in my resignation. Although he didn't say much, the look on his face said it all; he wasn't happy. He asked me not to tell anyone else until the big boss had a chance to speak with me. After anxiously waiting for a few days, I was finally summoned to the director's office. Naïve, I was totally unprepared for what happened next. This previously genial man turned irate and admonished me for wanting to leave. During his tirade, he reminded me that I was lucky to have a job at such a large and prestigious company. He continued to question my ability to succeed in the cutthroat world of consulting, especially since I had only a few months of experience behind me. He tried every possible way to demean and dissuade me. When he realized I was unwavering, he angrily pointed to the door, never even shaking my hand or wishing me luck. I learned one important lesson that day: I would never be a boss like him. For all you BS managers out there, when someone resigns to try to improve their life, politely ask them if there's anything that can be done to change their mind. If not, shake their hand and wish them the best.

As I moved forward with my consulting career, I always kept in touch with my colleagues at the old company to see how things turned out for them. It wasn't long after my departure that the department went through a major downsizing which resulted in layoffs. Since my tenure with the company had been so short, I surely would have been one of the first to go. Years later, the company was purchased and the remaining employees were faced with relocation to keep their jobs. So in retrospect my "rash" decision to jump to a "temporary" job turned out to be a great move. Clearly a huge gamble like this doesn't work for everyone. Let's face it, if you have five children and a mortgage, it's not a good idea to jump to a four-month job with no guarantees. Understandably, this drastic move was successful for me because I was young, with few responsibilities, and at the beginning of my career. I use it to illustrate that you should never become too comfortable in your current position if you want to reach your true potential.

Another example comes from my time working as an employee in the travel industry. I was managing the development and implementation of a complex international finance system. Having been blessed with a highly qualified and motivated team, I had no doubt that this project was going to be successful. We started by creating a realistic and comprehensive project plan. We purposely front-loaded the schedule to ensure there was enough time for exhaustive testing at the end. Then we went to work.

Over the next year, requirements were refined, programs were written, and the system began to take shape. My team was awesome and all their hard work resulted in us tracking ahead of schedule. But unfortunately, we weren't the only ones working on this project. There were two other development groups responsible for associated systems that fed and received information from ours. As months passed, I noticed a distressing pattern: my team was totally dedicated to the goal, frequently working through lunch, and putting in many hours of unpaid overtime, while in contrast, the other teams were taking extended lunches and leaving on time. Although I was worried about their ability to meet the schedule, my peer managers assured me that they were in good shape. So I remained focused on what my team needed to accomplish, assuming that the other managers would do same. Then the unthinkable happened.

Every Monday I held a recurring meeting with my group leaders to review their cost and schedule actuals verses plans. One memorable morning, a project lead barged into my office prior to the meeting, frantically waving the budget reports he had just printed. He was in a panic because a huge portion of our budget money was gone! Despite his agitated demeanor, I assumed a computer error had caused the numbers to drop. I calmly walked out of my office and down the hallway to the systems support area so that I could show them the problem. Unbelievably, they confirmed that the data was accurate! Confused, I headed up to mahogany row for an explanation.

When I asked the VP what happened to my group's budget dollars, without even looking up she nonchalantly stated, "The other teams were running low on money, so I had no choice but to reallocate some of your underrun dollars to the managers who were over their budget." As you can imagine, this initiated a heated debate. She hadn't even given me a heads-up before making the change. My dedicated, hard-working, proficient team was going to pay for someone else's incompetence; they were being penalized for doing a good job. Was she kidding me? Despite my protests, she was unwavering in her decision. And little did she know that eventually I would be as well.

During the long walk back to my office, I wondered how I was going to inform my team of her decision. I knew that the news would be devastating and that they would become totally demotivated. But worse, I was now going to expose the fact that our VP was a BS manager who didn't have the guts to hold the other teams responsible for their ineptness. She never even thanked my group for a job well done. I was embarrassed for her and embarrassed for the company.

No surprise, my group meeting was a disaster. Every one of my teammates was proud of what they had accomplished and the fact that we were running under budget; as I explained the VP's decision, I watched the dismay register on their faces. One manager even asked me how the company leaders could ignore the incompetence of the other teams. I didn't know what to say.

This event precipitated an examination of conscience. Was this the type of company I could be happy working for in the long run? What kind of role model was this VP? Was this a BS company or just one BS VP?

A few months later, after a major project milestone was reached, I took action and called a friend who had been trying to woo me to his company. When I eventually handed my BS VP a resignation letter, she pantomimed banging her head on her desk. She didn't have to ask why I was leaving; she knew damn well.

Quitting your job is not always the right answer. It's just as important to know when you should stay and slog through the difficulties. So here's one more example.

As my career progressed in the electronics distribution industry, my boss, the CIO, began lobbying the higher-ups to promote me to a VP position. I was excited about this prospect and worked even harder to ensure that there was no doubt in anyone's mind that I was worthy of this title. However a few months later, he called me into his office and apprised me that he himself had just resigned for an opportunity at another company. I was devastated; he was the main reason I had joined the firm. He had been a great leader and an excellent role model, inspiring me to be just like him. Although I was extremely disappointed that he was leaving, I never imagined how negatively his move would ultimately affect me.

Weeks went by and candidates were interviewed for his job. In an attempt to settle down a jittery team, executive management decided that all of the CIO's direct reports should be part of the interview process for their prospective new boss. After meeting with several candidates, I actually felt encouraged that my next C would be a good one. Eventually, the new CIO was hired. He seemed smart and fair, and the organization proceeded to hum along as normal. Then it happened….

Toward the end of a busy day, my boss's assistant called and asked if I could fit in a last-minute interview with a potential new employee. Of course I agreed, but didn't know the details of the position for which the person was being considered. With no time to prepare, I picked up the résumé and headed into one of the conference rooms. A really nice guy entered and introduced himself. As we spent the next hour discussing his credentials and experience, I decided that he was terrific; we shared many of the same views on teamwork, motivation, and technology. Before he was escorted away, I nonchalantly asked him an innocent question, "Hey, what position are you interviewing for?" When he answered, my heart sunk – it was the VP slot I was promised!

I was the last person of the day to meet with him. Once I finished, the CIO convened the entire team in his office. Every one of my peers sitting around the table was asked by our new boss what we thought of the potential new VP…who just happened to be his friend from his prior company. No one in the room would make eye contact with me; they all knew I was about to get screwed. When it was my turn to give an evaluation, I said, "The guy is awesome. You need to hire him." Everyone was shocked! I continued listing his accomplishments, honestly complimenting him along the way.

Once the meeting ended, I walked into my office and immediately called the prior CIO, my friend and supporter who had just recently moved to another company. He straightaway arranged for me to interview at his new corporation the following week. And I got the job.

When I handed in my resignation, the you know what hit the fan. The C's all wanted to meet with me. Again, I was asked to keep quiet until they had finished working me over. During the next two weeks I learned another important lesson: top executives are used to getting exactly what they want. I was offered an immediate raise, that VP job, and more responsibility. However, it was very difficult to get past the emotional hurt and betrayal, so I was determined to make them pay by leaving the company. I pretty much had my mind made up until they sent in their secret weapon.

One of the top corporate executives flew back from her vacation specifically to meet with me. Not only was she well-respected within the company, she had a sterling reputation throughout the entire industry. She was one of the executives that I had trusted and admired. We discussed my future as we ate lunch in her office. I informed her that I wouldn't be comfortable accepting a pay raise, a title change or anything else based solely on my resignation. That's when she offered me something else, something even more valuable: she volunteered to become my mentor.

So I kept my old title and stayed. This was one of the best career decisions I ever made. She was incredibly smart and someone I knew I could learn from. I realized that I didn't want money; I wanted opportunity. I quickly headed back to my office and called my old boss. Having worked with my new mentor himself, he agreed that it was a chance of a lifetime and conceded that I made the right decision.

By the way, the new CIO's friend that I had interviewed for "my" VP job turned down the position he was offered because he decided that he didn't want to live on the East Coast. I was eventually awarded that VP title; but more importantly, I was given exactly what I wanted: the opportunity to prove myself.

Admittedly, the above three examples are extreme. They took place over a twenty-five-year career and weren't common events. However they all demonstrate the value of not getting so comfortable in your current position that you would never have the courage to leave. You are the CEO of your career and you must manage it with great care. Stay in touch with colleagues from prior jobs, attend training and conferences to hone your professional and technical skills, and continue to challenge yourself to learn new things.

Obviously the answer to every difficulty at work is not to get up and leave. My point is that you should constantly be preparing and working toward your next job, whether it's within your current company or at another. Many of the C's I've observed devote an extraordinary amount of time training and networking for their next position. In contrast, the "real workers" spend little time doing the same and are often caught off guard when their work environment unexpectedly changes.

"In the past a leader was a boss. Today's leaders must be partners with their people... they no longer can lead solely based on positional power."
Ken Blanchard, author

CHAPTER 2
It All Starts at the Top

Company culture starts at the top. We've all read unbelievable stories about the CEO who pillaged his shareholders by expensing $6,000 shower curtains and $15,000 umbrella stands. Or, how about the CEO who was accused of sexual harassment by a famous actress, or another one resigning because he lied about his connection with a male escort service. There was a CEO who committed accounting fraud and one who engaged in illegal stock trades involving a Canadian porn star, no less. It takes a special kind of CEO to lie about degrees from a bible college of all places or the one who actually drove himself to prison in his Mercedes. I assure you that all of these examples are true.

But, awesomeness does exist! I want to be clear; there are many remarkable companies and remarkable people in the corporate world. Since any company is a direct reflection of its leaders, here are a few stories about the incredible executives I've had the pleasure of working for.

Late one Sunday evening, I was working with a large team of people who were exhaustively testing a new complex system. I was surprised when I heard my phone ring and saw from the display that it was one of our company's top executives. She requested that I come up to her office and explain how the project was going. During our conversation, she asked if I had a photo of the team. I quickly jogged back to my desk and grabbed one of the many integration team pictures, then returned to her office. She spent the next half hour carefully studying the photo and asking me questions about the people. She not only wrote down each person's name, but also noted what they were responsible for. Then I was excused and went back to work.

An hour later, she appeared in our area and I watched as she walked up to each person, greeted them by name, shook their hand, and thanked them for their specific contribution to the project. This was a really big deal! When she eventually finished and made her way back to her office, I was besieged by gladdened and reenergized teammates who were amazed that she knew so much about them. A little appreciation certainly went a long way, especially to a group of employees who were giving it their all. As Mark Twain said, *"I can live for two months on a good compliment."* I can attest that this is absolutely true because I witnessed the effect on my overworked team. I really hadn't been surprised by this exec's actions because she'd demonstrated extraordinary leadership for years.

So tell me, when was the last time you had a senior executive take hours out of their weekend to get to know individual contributor's names, just so they could be thanked? For those of you BS types saying, "Well, she should have already known their names," let me further explain: this was a multibillion-dollar, Fortune 150 company, with offices worldwide, and tens of thousands of employees!

Here's another example: On one of my business trips, I left from New York, went to Tokyo, then onto Hong

28

Kong, Singapore, Bangalore, Mumbai, Paris, and eventually back home. The amazing part of this around the world journey was that wherever I went, no matter how remote, the people had actually met our CEO! When I entered one of our tiny offices in Bangalore, India, I was shocked to see the CEO's picture hanging in the entryway. Joking around, I asked if they had printed it off the internet. When I was told that our CEO had not only visited this location, but spent time with each of the handful of people who worked there, I was amazed.

Another quick story (hey, I warned you in the introduction!). I was asked by my boss, the CIO, if I would travel with him to a remote warehouse in the midwestern United States. Although I was happy to accompany him, I didn't see how this trip related to the work I was currently doing. When I asked him about it, he said, "This trip is not about your current job, but as you gain more responsibility, it could very well be related to your next job." Imagine that someone other than me was actually thinking about my future. In retrospect, I now see that this was just one of the signs of what a great boss he was, a true leader. This made me even more excited to go.

Corporate BS

So we made our way to a rural area out west. Almost all of the employees in this warehouse were wives whose husbands worked as farmers; the main reason the women had taken these jobs was to get health benefits for their families. After our meetings were done, we took a guided tour of the warehouse. This is when I saw my boss shine. He initiated conversation with every worker we encountered, not only discussing their specific responsibilities, but their husbands' jobs as well. These dedicated employees were smiling and animated as they engaged with him. I remember running through the airport; we almost missed our return flight because my boss wouldn't leave until he had a chance to thank every single individual who worked in that facility. I may not have learned a lot about warehousing that day, but I learned something far more important: those employees we left behind were now energized, inspired, and even more committed to the company and their jobs…all because my great boss took the time to simply meet and thank them.

Although I never considered myself a great leader compared to the other people I exemplify in this book,

I'd like to share one more personal story where a trivial action on my part unintentionally motivated my team.

During a multibillion-dollar merger project in the distribution sector, I challenged a few of the senior team members to devise a way to print the new electronic warehouse labels prior to the conversion with a view toward reducing computer system downtime and overall conversion risk. These well-meaning technicians immediately protested that it couldn't be done. Unfazed, I politely requested that they nevertheless indulge me and discuss the issue with some of the system experts over the next few days. If they all reached consensus that it couldn't be done, I would be willing to accept the answer.

When our subsequent team meeting took place, they excitedly told me that not only did they come up with a solution; it turned out that it really wouldn't be very hard to implement. Weeks later, we were ready to print the new bar code labels. The only problem was that the antiquated contraption that produced them needed to be manned full time, a monotonous and mind-numbing task. We were set to begin printing labels in the afternoon, but no one on the team could realistically spare the time to babysit the machine since they were extremely busy with other critical project priorities. When they asked who was going to have the dreaded task of folding the tags as they were produced, I said, "Don't worry…I'll figure it out."

I walked back to my office, canceled my afternoon meetings, hung up my suit jacket and removed my tie (remember when we used to dress up at work?). Over the next three and a half hours, I sat in a chair and folded hundreds of labels. As word spread throughout our building, people began walking by just to catch a glance of me doing this tedious piecework. It was fun in a strange sort of way. Eventually, even a few of the executives walked over to add their support.

This simple unplanned act was talked about for weeks. But more importantly, it set the tone for the entire project. Suddenly, everyone was willing to do the most mundane and previously unwelcomed tasks — anything to make the project a success. A BS manager would never have lowered himself to do such an insignificant job. On the contrary, non-BS managers will accept any task to get the job done.

Tim Tebow has said, *"I didn't want to be like everyone else. I wanted to be better. If I did what everybody else did, then why would you look up to me? Why would I set an example?"*

As a manager, you're always on display. Your example is often imitated by your subordinates. So, if you have a poor work ethic (like taking extra-long lunches), you can expect your team to do the same.

"Telling the truth and making someone cry is better than telling a lie and making someone smile."
Paola Coehlo, novelist

CHAPTER 3
You Want the Truth? You Can't Handle the Truth!

With coaching from my new mentor, I was eventually appointed to a lead position on a complex corporate restructuring project. Company presidents were being assigned to new business segments based on product lines. This required that all of the supporting computer systems and internal processes be modified; a herculean task! Although anxious to succeed, I have to admit that I was a bit nervous and wondered if it could all get done within the aggressive time frame.

A few months into the project, I was scheduled to attend a meeting in the board room. This was nothing new for me. However I usually sat in the row of chairs positioned along the wall (you know, the "bleachers"); but now, because of the magnitude of this project, I was actually sitting at the table with the C's and company presidents. Eventually I was asked to give the status of my portion of the realignment project. No problem. When I finished, the CEO thanked me and then proceeded to describe a new shared commission system that he wanted us to implement; he had a high-level vision for how it should work and what it should do. No problem. But then he turned to me and directed that the new system needed to be developed and implemented without impacting our original schedule. Say whaaat?

Assuming that this was business as usual, all the presidents prepared to move on to the next agenda item, but I interrupted them, "We can't get that done." I watched as everyone put down their pens and stared at me in disbelief. I knew what they were all thinking, "Is this rookie really telling the CEO 'no'?" Surprised, but not dissuaded, the CEO rebutted, "It's as simple as adding a column to a spreadsheet."

Listen, I wasn't afraid of hard work, nor was I one of those "it's not in the schedule so we can't do it" kind of managers. My whole reputation was based on being the reliable can-do anything employee. If the execs wanted it, I always prided myself on making it happen. Heck, that's why they chose me to run this huge monstrosity.

But this was different. I uneasily replied, "It's much more than just adding a column. There will be a ripple effect across all the systems that are already in the middle of being changed for the realignment. I don't care about the re-work; I care about the risk." Silence filled the room. Undeterred, he challenged, "I know you can pull this off."

I stammered, "No, I don't think you want us to jeopardize the entire project for one change. Maybe instead we can create some work-around reports, or do something manually until the systems are stable." He seemed to be enjoying the debate as he looked at me over his reading glasses and taunted, "But you'll get a big bonus if you get this done."

I took a really deep breath and replied, "I don't think it's worth the risk." Without another word, he moved on to the next item. Eventually the meeting ended and I'll never forget the walk back to my office. Each president who passed me in the hallway said the same thing, "I can't believe you did that." I collapsed into my desk chair and wondered if I had just committed career suicide. I actually thought about taking my photos and personal items home just in case I wasn't coming back.

After a sleepless night, I arrived at work early the next morning. As soon as I got to my desk, the phone rang. Looking at the display, my heart sank; it read extension 1600, the president's office (just like the White House). I answered with trepidation, but it wasn't the CEO; it was his right-hand person, the COO, my mentor. She asked me what I was doing that afternoon. Not fully understanding the question and wondering if I still had a job, I innocently replied, "Working on the realignment project, I think?" She asked if I would be able to attend a meeting with the CEO on supply chain integration. I reminded her that I was no expert on the subject and then questioned, "Why does he want me at the meeting?" She replied, "Because he knows you'll tell him the truth." Her answer proved I made the correct choice in that board room yesterday. That meeting changed my career. From then on, the CEO knew he could always count on me for one thing: an honest opinion. If this were a BS company, I would have been removed from the team for defying the

CEO's wishes, not celebrated with additional responsibility. This admirable CEO demonstrated that he didn't want BS; he wanted the truth.

Another particularly challenging time in my career came after the company I worked for purchased a controlling interest in a midwestern computer distribution firm. Shortly after the public announcement, I was on an airplane for our first full meeting with the executives responsible for the integration of the systems and processes. Once the overview was presented, I could tell that not everyone was happy with the project plan. After a somewhat heated debate on everything from the project timeline to the extent of system changes required, the entire crew of senior executives from the purchased company, including its CEO, stood up in unison and walked out! My team and I were left sitting alone in a strange conference room, wondering how to proceed. I really didn't know what to do, but I knew one thing for sure: I wasn't leaving.

Over the next few days, we continued working without them. When the executives finally returned, I invited the CEO to join me for lunch. He unenthusiastically agreed and curtly informed me that he would be bringing his right hand person with him. I could tell that he was looking for a fight. I patiently listened to this C's complaints (a few admittedly valid) over and over again as we ignored our food. After hearing the same repetitive list of insults for about the fifth time, I respectfully interrupted and asked if he would like to know what I thought. When he reluctantly acquiesced, my words of frustration came spewing out. You may remember newscaster Howard Beale's passionate "I'm as mad as hell, and I'm not going to take this anymore!" speech in the movie Network. Well, I launched into my own Howard Beale type of rant. I vividly remember that I ended with a sentence that went something like this: "I truly believe that if you would just put as much effort into making this project successful as you have already done by trying to make it fail, we would have addressed your overall concerns, and we'd be well on our way toward creating an implementation plan that would make us all happy." There was silence. Even though I was passionate, I made sure to deliver my tirade respectfully. I didn't know how he was going to react; it could have gone either way. To my amazement, the C finally nodded his head gravely and looked at the executive sitting next to him, "He's right!" Whew. We spent the rest of the day together making plans on the best way to engage his team and make the project a success. Once again, the CEO didn't want BS; he wanted the truth.

"Illusion is needed to disguise the emptiness within."
Arthur Erickson, architect

CHAPTER 4
Characters in the Corporate Screenplay

It's all about the people. Although we can't always choose our coworkers, subordinates or bosses, it's critical to recognize the types of people we're working with. Some are a good influence; others are toxic. If you don't want to be considered a BS employee or BS manager, you need carefully navigate amongst the bad ones.

Each time I took on a new position, I spent a considerable amount of time closely observing the players both above and below me. In my own Dilbert way, I developed different categories to identify the untrustworthy people within the organization. And then I tried to steer around them.

Let's start with the Parrots. I bet you're already nodding in agreement. These are people who never seem to have an original idea, but are great at repeating anyone else's. They steal an observation from others while pretending it's their own. Here's an example:

In the interim before a new CIO was hired, I had been running the weekly international status meeting, a conference call with directors from around the world. The new guy was eventually appointed and during his first week of work, I was summoned to his office an hour before the first of these meetings that he was scheduled to attend. No time for niceties, he got right to the point. Understandably, I was drilled on every single detail from the prior calls. He systematically documented my words with great precision. When we were finished, we started from the top of his list and reviewed it all again. Right before we dialed-in to the call, he informed me that he would be the one speaking and that I should remain silent. Getting the hint, as the call connected, I respectfully mouthed if he just wanted me to leave his office; he shook his head violently and motioned for me to stay. As the meeting progressed, I listened as he parroted back my exact words from the prior hour; he didn't even try to change them! He authoritatively spouted out all of my observations regarding the various systems, along with my suggestions as to how we should move forward with the development projects. Not once did he ever attribute these ideas to me. If I didn't know any better, I would have thought I was listening to myself speak. When a manager from Germany deviated from the agenda and asked a question regarding an unscheduled topic, I saw the CIO's eyes widen in panic. He understandably didn't know how to answer, but I was unsure if he wanted me to reveal my presence by jumping in. After stumbling for a few seconds, he impatiently motioned to me. Still hesitant and not wanting to break the imposed vow of silence, I put my hand over the speaker and whispered, "Do you want me to answer?" With no time to transcribe my words and repeat them, he reluctantly nodded. Everyone on the call was surprised to hear my voice. By the time I returned to my desk, I had several emails calling my new boss an idiot. What he should have done was let me lead the call, but then ask his own probing questions and jump in where he felt he could contribute. He should have been open about his lack of familiarity with the topics while expressing a sincere desire to learn. Then he would have been admired, not condemned. Was he really so insecure that he felt he had to assume the "I'm the big-boss" persona from the get-go? What a mistake.

And don't think Parrots are only found in management; subordinates can be Parrots too. These BS employees are really more like vultures, picking over everyone else's good ideas and hoping to get credit for them. Try to be conscious of Parrots regardless if they're at the bottom or the top of the organization; BS has no boundaries. The only respect that's worthwhile is respect based on not misrepresenting yourself.

Next up, the Actors. Yes, right from my desk I've witnessed Oscar-worthy performances in the corporate world. I bet you have too. These guys love being on stage. You know, the ones who call a meeting just so they can bask in the spotlight at the head of the table with a captive audience. We've all seen executives who gravely proclaim their philosophy about how important "people" are to the organization, but in reality, they wouldn't be able to name one person lower than a director. They pronounce the value of being a corporate "family" and then commit to unrealistic deadlines that require those "family members" to work unconscionable hours, on holidays, with no regard for the prolonged impact on their real families. These are the guys that know the bartender at the local golf course better than the manager at the local sales office. Actors are the worst kind of managers because they know that they are being disingenuous, but they do it anyway. They don't realize that people in the organization are savvy and can spot a phony a mile away. So it's better for the Actor not to say anything than to spew a bunch of BS that totally demotivates their troops. If you're an Actor, you're a BS manager. And a BS manager is going to get BS results.

Ever encounter a Chameleon? You already know who we're talking about. These are the folks who will change their stripes at a moment's notice. They'll do anything just to fit in and get ahead. Brownnosing the higher-ups is the order of the day. Maybe it entails wearing the same style of clothes, or nodding in agreement after the boss' every word; whatever it takes to kiss-up. I've even witnessed employees buying the same model of new car as their boss (you think I'm kidding, right?). Here's a real-life example that probably seems unbelievable:

I worked with a senior manager who was an avid NY Jets football fan. He proudly wore their team jersey on dress-down day and his office was filled with Jets memorabilia. Any competing NY Giants fan had to endure his good-natured ribbing. Then we got a new boss who happened to be a Giant's fan. Funny how all the manager's Jet stuff gradually disappeared from his office. And no surprise, he eventually came to work wearing a Giant's jersey. Could it have gotten any more blatant?

More importantly, these Chameleons change their work views at a moment's notice to match those of anyone they're trying to impress. Don't they realize that they're fooling no one? You'll be more respected if you're secure in your own beliefs than by capriciously reflecting the views of others.

Hopefully these examples will help you identify the BS employees in your own corporate screenplay so you can maneuver around them. Sometimes it's like navigating a mine field. Forewarned is forearmed.

"Words are singularly the most powerful force available to humanity. We can choose to use this force constructively with words of encouragement, or destructively using words of despair. Words have energy and power with the ability to help, to heal, to hinder, to hurt, to harm, to humiliate and to humble."
Yehuda Berg, author

CHAPTER 5
The Inmates are Running the Asylum

During my career at various companies, there were many instances when I had to work closely with representatives from the Human Resources (HR) department. From gathering user requirements for new systems, to implementing promotions or special training for my staff, most of my interactions with people from within this organization were pleasant and productive. However, sometimes HR operates as if it is a leadership organization rather than a support organization. Let's start with the Employee Performance Review (EPR) process.

As a manager, I dreaded the annual EPR process. It wasn't that I was unwilling to assess my employees or discuss their performance; I didn't mind the work at all and I welcomed the opportunity for formal coaching. I just didn't like the BS that went along with it. Understandably, all corporate managers were required to submit ratings of their personnel. That part was fine. However, what happened a few weeks later was a nightmare. The HR group would consolidate all of the ratings and run "statistics." Then countless absurd meetings would take place to tell you how your ratings (which you had carefully considered and developed) needed to change. The narrative sounded something like this: "You have x many high performers and it's throwing off our performance Bell Curve." Yeah, so? I get the fact that a team is typically comprised of employees at all levels of competence — you know, the cream of the crop rises to the top and the rest level out below. However, sometimes I was blessed to be leading a team of all top performers who'd been hand-picked to work on a particularly challenging and grueling project. Let's face it, when some hot new system with a deadline from hell had to be developed, we looked at each organization and raided the top tier. Despite this reality, these HR professionals insisted that I lower my team's ratings because they were forced to comply with the company's strict policies. They didn't even know the people whose lives they were affecting. It was just a mindless numbers game they were required to achieve.

To make it even worse, one company I worked for insisted that every employee needed to be rated a "2" (i.e., under-performing, or as it was titled on the form, "Somewhat Below Others") in at least one of five predetermined categories. The CEO who implemented this rule was one of the best I've ever worked for and I give him credit because he submitted himself to the same scrutiny from the Board of Directors. But I never understood how telling your best performers that they were "Below Others" motivated them.

As a manager, I never shied away from rating someone a "2" if they deserved it since we all have areas that need improvement. I was concerned that telling someone that they were "Below Others" would just foster an atmosphere of distrust and non-cooperation among team members. I would have preferred that the "2" rating be called "Area Needs Improvement." Although I would always make an effort to explain the hurtful words away, I understood how it made my subordinates feel, because I felt the same way when I received my own review.

These labels didn't motivate anyone; instead they created a competitive environment since the employee was told in writing (and on their permanent company record) that they were below their peers. Once that happened, employees would sit at their desks, narrow their eyes and look around, trying to identify who was better than them in their worst category. This is just one example of how supposedly good-intentioned processes inadvertently pitted peers against peers, inevitably destroying the cohesive team mentality that's critical to business success. Highly competitive people are asked to work together, but then they are constantly being compared to each other for performance ratings, raises, and their share of the bonus pool. Instead of teamwork, this fosters a cutthroat mentality – an "every man out for himself" scenario. Here's a great illustration of this:

I once attended a conference where I watched an on-stage presentation that I'll never forget. The late, great author Stephen Covey, best known for the book, *The Seven Habits of Highly Effective People*, stood in front of a packed auditorium and asked for two volunteers. After lots of audience hands went up, he walked around and carefully selected one very large, muscular man and another very slightly-built one. These guinea pigs made their way onto the stage and Stephen motioned for them to sit in chairs on opposite ends of a small table. He then announced to the crowd that the men were going to arm wrestle. Stephen instructed the players to continue the competition for a full minute while he kept score. Every time one of them won, they'd be given a dollar. A buzzer sounded and the combatants struggled. They would grapple for 10–20 seconds, but then the big guy would inevitably pin the smaller man's hand. The same scene happened several times until the buzzer finally rang again. Mr. Covey retrieved his wallet and handed the winner a few bucks. But before the two competitors could return to their seats, Stephen sat opposite the huge man and they locked hands. However, before beginning their duel, he whispered some words in his ear. The bell sounded and surprisingly each one took turns pinning the other's arm in 1–2 seconds, with both men quickly winning over and over again. When the buzzer rang this time, each man was due to receive over twenty-five dollars! Good one, right? This vivid demonstration of teamwork is forged in my memory. In the competitive corporate environment, aren't we often arm wrestling and looking for individual wins?

Now, let's get back to the EPR process and dig a little deeper into the ugly underbelly of HR's version of the game. Eventually changes to employee ratings would ultimately be determined by peer mangers sitting in conference rooms and trying to determine, as a team, whose EPR rating was going to be lowered. This process often involved reviewing data on hundreds of people. When everyone was tired of arguing, and as the deadline approached, concessions would be made. As a last-ditch effort to mold the collective ratings into the sacred Bell Curve, the discussion would almost always end with an interesting, if appalling, question: "Do you think that he/she will resign if they get a low rating?" So what happened?

Employees who were thought of as unlikely to quit (often single mothers or long-term, older employees), were punished by having their rating lowered to help the combined numbers "look better." *Seriously?*

Chapter 1 described the importance of being the CEO of your career. In addition, you must also be the CMO or Chief Marketing Officer of your career. If your boss doesn't take the time to do a good job promoting your value to the company, you better do it yourself! Wait; don't get the wrong idea. It doesn't mean that you should spend your days advertising your accomplishments to anyone who will listen; who would want to be around an employee like that? But you should provide your boss with enough information, through status reports and other forms of documentation, so that your worth to the organization is evident.

One boss I worked for had his direct reports write their own performance reviews. He would then take our words and reformat them while adding his own comments. Although I thought this was a cop-out on his part, it was easy for me because I maintained an informal spreadsheet where I continually jotted down my particularly grueling tasks and accomplishments (it only took a few minutes a week to do). When these successes were backed up with facts and figures, they were hard to ignore. I knew my manager was forced to find a category to rate me "Somewhat Below Others," but I wanted it to be a struggle.

I've worked with many extremely smart individuals who never took the time to document their value because they were "just too busy." They were so caught up in the minute-to-minute workday problems (which let's face it, always exist), that they took their eyes off the big picture.

These employees sabotaged their careers, not because they weren't smart, but because they naively trusted that their boss had their best interests in mind. That's a mistake. Think about it from your boss' perspective: he or she probably has lots of direct reports and it's easy to forget some of their individual accomplishments. Why not help them?

As a subordinate myself, I was always sensitive to this issue. So when I became a manager and had to write performance evaluations for my staff, I would always review their detailed status reports that were submitted over the last review cycle in order to ensure that I was capturing their accomplishments. I'm not trying to tell you that I was a perfect manager, far from it, but my intention was to be fair.

The following demonstrates how important employee documentation can be.

A VP had brought a director with him from a prior company and a few years later during corporate reorganization he was transferred to my team. He seemed like a great worker and I'd only heard good things about my new direct report. After working for me for about three months, it was decided that the company needed to downsize; people had to be laid off. While meeting to determine the unfortunate candidates, my new employee's old boss (the VP who brought him to our company) spoke up and directed that I fire his recruit. I was shocked to hear this. Having done my homework, I had all of his past performance reviews summarized, including the ones his VP betrayer had written. Once presented with the data, along with a recent email from a company president complementing this employee, my peers quickly moved onto other candidates.

As a manager, I took the marketing aspect of my job very seriously, not only because it would benefit me as an individual, but because I hoped it would also increase exposure for my entire team. Let's face it, where would I be without them? Nowhere. I made sure that subordinates were in a position to shine. I submitted status reports that were extremely informative, with executive summaries up front and details following. Included in the report were the specific names of individuals who were responsible for achieving a particular goal or milestone. My boss always knew where we stood on projects. It encouraging how much data your boss will consume if your provide it! I often invited key personnel to present project status in the board room so that they would get recognition.

During large projects, I was fastidious about keeping statistics; I tracked everything from the number of plane trips taken by the team, to the number of lines of computer code that were added to the systems. From the total number of real estate consolidations, to the amount of customer numbers converted. From the hundreds of White Castle hamburgers ordered during one weekend to demonstrate how many hours were being worked (really) to the amount of inventory dollars converted. I measured everything. My goal was to ensure that the executive committee was in a position to fully appreciate the sacrifices that the team was making. And there was another important reason I did this: when it came time to award the generous project completion bonuses, I didn't want anyone to question the amount of work that had been done by a particular person.

So getting back to those ridiculous HR EPR meetings, I always had enough undeniable evidence about my team and their accomplishments to limit the capricious performance rating changes. Many times my peers, the ones who were "just too busy" to write things down, couldn't provide the same level of detailed documentation, and their teams suffered the consequences.

I cannot stress enough that my success in the corporate world was directly related to the wonderful teams I had the opportunity to work with. A great piece of advice I received was when I was promoted to my very first management position. My boss called me in his office and told me something very important: "You've been promoted to a manager, so you've been recognized. Now it's your job is to ensure your team gets credit for their accomplishments. That's your new job." This was an important lesson to learn and it helped me control the inmates who were running the asylum.

"There are no extra pieces in the universe. Everyone is here because he or she has a place to fill, and every piece must fit itself into the big jigsaw puzzle."
Deepak Chopra, author

CHAPTER 6
Every Peg has Its Hole

During my later years in corporate America, I worked on mergers and acquisitions in the electronics distribution sector. Once a company was purchased, I lead the teams who integrated the computer systems, consolidated real estate, mapped the financials, and developed the combined operational procedures. It was an extremely challenging job, with high-stakes deadlines; but it was the best job I ever had. In many cases the purchased company's senior level managers were assured of a future job, a huge payout, or both. But it was widely conceded that once the acquisition announcement was made, the lower level employees, who live the lesson in Chapter 1 in this book, would immediately become worried and start calling their friends about other job opportunities.

In order to protect the most important asset of any company, the people, critical decisions had to be made very quickly in order to quell any nervousness within the ranks. For example, no one wanted the top sales people (who are continually recruited by competitors) to leave, taking their high-dollar customers with them. So in an attempt to calm the workforce of the acquired company by limiting the time of uncertainty, our corporate acquisition teams started working on the details of the process, organizational, and system consolidations in secret, prior to the public announcement. This meant quickly scrambling to assemble "special ops" teams that were guaranteed to contain the myriad of skills required to take the acquisition from the gleam in the CEO's eye to actual implementation.

During this controlled chaos, my job was to fit the pieces of the puzzle together, i.e., to ensure that every person was in the best possible position for overall project success. This is where it got challenging. The only way to be assured that the right people were chosen for these "A Teams" was to already have an in-depth knowledge of their particular strengths. For my managers on the team, it meant having the confidence that they knew the capabilities of the staff below them.

I truly believe that most employees want to do a good job and it's management's responsibility to find the role that fits them bet. When someone puts forth an honest effort with everything they have, but still fails, it's almost always because they're in the wrong position. I spent a lot of time trying to get to know my people so that when they struggled, I'd be able to help.

In sports, all of the pieces have to fit together to win a championship. Success is pure and measurable; people keep score. No one talks their way onto the field; the stats tell the story. Check out National Basketball Association Hall of Famer Charles Barkley's golf swing online. It's terrible! Better yet, it's abysmal! But no one could ever ague that he wasn't a great athlete. Often, we hand someone on our staff a nine iron, when we should be throwing them a basketball. Ever hear of Hunter Pence? If you have, I bet you're smiling. Hunter played outfield for the San Francisco Giants. Here's how Giant's blogger Grant Brisbee describes him: *"Runs like a rotary phone thrown into a running clothes dryer. Throws like an effete Frenchman throwing a bookcase uphill. Swings a bat like his elbows are stapled to his knees and his underwear is pulled over his head. Stares at you while you aren't looking."* Yet, this guy was one of the best baseball players on the planet. How about golf? Lee Trevino has one of the most unorthodox swings ever. Yet, this man has won six major championships over the course of his career. He's one of only four players to twice win the U.S. Open, the Open Championship and the PGA Championship. Truly amazing for someone who looks like he's going to fall down when he swings a club.

In the corporate world, sometimes we're more concerned about the way "the swing" looks, rather than results. If these athletes were judged on anything but performance, they'd be considered a failure. One of the keys to my success was that I had many teams made up of incredibly smart and talented people with ugly swings. I actually searched the organization for these people! I call them Ugly Ducklings. These are frequently the most underappreciated and underrated employees in an organization. I'll explain.

I've encountered many great professionals who just didn't fit into the corporate image. Perhaps they were verbally abrupt or physically unpolished. This often caused them to be undeservedly ostracized to the second string. I'm thankful that I had the opportunity to discover these diamonds in the rough. Here's a story about one of them.

An employee I inherited on a new team was a tough character to work with. Although he wasn't abusive or downright rude, he definitely lacked people skills. Others who communicated with him couldn't stand his delivery, which was extremely direct and to the point. The guy had no patience for stupid questions or idle talk; he was all about the work. But his knowledge of the business was unparalleled. Whenever we had major system problems, he was the one to figure it out. I came to rely on him and his expertise in critical situations. He became my go-to guy and obviously deserved a higher title. Curious as to why his previous managers hadn't promoted him, I reviewed his past performance reviews. No surprise, I found that his prior boss had skewed his evaluation by only focusing on his communication weaknesses, never acknowledging his technical strengths. I ended up promoting the guy and coaching him on how to improve his rapport with his coworkers.

I've watched many ugly ducklings relegated to the bench so that a new "shiny penny" could be hired who knew nothing about the business. It took years for these green employees to become productive, and many times they had to rely on the ugly duckling that they replaced for training before eventually displaying a hitch in their own swing. Don't discount Ugly Ducklings; coach them. They're often the hidden gems in the organization. Songwriter, David Allan Coe said, *"It is not the beauty of a building you should look at; it's the construction of the foundation that will stand the test of time."*

In addition to recognizing an employee's skills, a good manager must also realize that understanding an employee's motivation, i.e., why they come to work, is critical to determining their best fit within the team. I had an employee who I thought was never overly-motivated since he left work exactly on time, on the dot, every single afternoon. One Christmas Eve, I was surprised to run into him at a local hospital while I was visiting a sick relative. He explained that his mother-in-law was terminally ill and that he came to the hospital to feed her every night. Boy, didn't I feel foolish for erroneously casting him as an uninterested worker. So he may have not been the most productive employee in the world, but he certainly was the best son-in-law. I had chalked up his lack of concentration and attentiveness to a lazy attitude; but now I understood the reason; he had other, more important, priorities. Once I realized the situation, I immediately found a better hole for this peg. Because of his preoccupation with non-work issues, he was extremely satisfied doing mundane tasks that no one else wanted to do (like comparing relatively boring reports). I needed someone to do that and he fit the bill. It was a win-win for both of us.

You can't prevail with all superstars; there often aren't enough superstar tasks to keep them all interested and motivated. When assembling teams, it's critical to remember that if you place an overachiever into a role that's not challenging, you've created an unhappy employee.

And just because the peg fits in the hole, doesn't guarantee success. The type of hole must also be considered. You may think that now I'm splitting hairs, but as you will see, one mistake can be extremely costly.

New York Met fans will probably remember when Bobby Bonilla was signed as a free agent to a five-year, $29 million contract based on his phenomenal success with the Pirates. This new deal made him the highest paid player in the league at the time. But the constant pressure from the notoriously mean-spirited NY media seemed to have a detrimental effect on his performance. After four less than impressive seasons, the Mets traded him. Bobby went on to help the Orioles get to the American League Champion Series and then was an important part of the World Series winning Florida Marlins team. So he was very successful, but not in the NY market with its added stress caused by unrelenting press scrutiny and fan pressure. In what some call the worst financial settlement in baseball history, the Mets wound up deferring a large portion of his salary as part of a subsequent deal that pays him $1.2 million until 2035. All this for a player who didn't perform.

Successful hiring just may be the most difficult challenge in the corporate world. So many factors must be considered. Sometimes it might be worth training and coaching the people you already employ because you understand their shortcomings. It's a gamble to search for a new superman who may find that your particular work environment doesn't fit their personality or it's loaded with kryptonite.

When you're a manager, you're the architect of your team. It's your job to mold and shape them while ensuring that they are in not only the best possible position to succeed, but to flourish. Because of this, every time someone on your staff fails, you fail too. If you can construct a team with the right people in the right roles, everything else usually falls into place. BS managers who build teams on unstable foundations shouldn't be surprised when the structure inevitably crumbles.

"The way a team plays as a whole determines its success. You may have the greatest bunch of individual stars in the world, but if they don't play together, the club won't be worth a dime."
Babe Ruth,— baseball great

CHAPTER 7
Playing Nice in the Sandbox

An important ingredient for success is an environment where teamwork flourishes. A manager's approach and example are critical to creating a cohesive group.

I always tried to make sure that regardless of their tasks, every team member felt that they were critical to the group's success — no favorites. If I noticed that someone was being ostracized by their peers, I would invite them to lunch with his or her teammates and make sure that everyone was part of the conversation. If I observed that two team members were at odds, I would purposely assign them to a project where they had to work closely together, knowing that by the end of it, they'd have a better appreciation for each other. Some of the deepest business bonds I've forged were developed because of an immense struggle endured with someone I had previously disliked.

After one particular departmental reorganization I ended up with some subordinate directors who had never before worked with me or for me. After a few weeks of interacting as a team, one of them entered my office and started to complain about a peer. Not aware of my management style, he was clearly surprised when mid-conversation (or should I say mid-complaint), I picked up the phone and dialed an extension. As I waited for the recipient to answer, he quizzically asked who I was calling. I calmly explained that if he was going to grumble about someone on our team, then that person had a right to hear the complaint so that they could defend themselves. Of course being face-to-face with the target of his dissatisfaction was a whole different ballgame. As New Jersey Governor Chris Christie said, *"It's hard to hate up close."* I facilitated a civilized conversation between the two of them and they successfully resolved their issues. As you can guess, no one ever came into my office again to offhandedly grouse about another without first having tried to settle the issue without me. After all, these were directors, not low-level employees; they should be capable of parenting themselves.

In business and politics, a critical ingredient for success is to be able to work with people you wouldn't invite to your house for dinner. I always tried to remind myself to focus on a person's strengths, not their weaknesses. President Bill Clinton is quoted as saying, *"He used to call me twice a year in his second term just to talk. We'd talk depending on how much time he had, somewhere between 30 and 45 minutes for several years. He asked my opinion. Half the time he disagreed with it."* Who would have guessed that he was referring to President George W. Bush! If these two political arch rivals were able to find common ground, anyone can.

On large projects, I attempted to combat the standard mentality of rewards based solely on one particular team's achievements by changing the bonus criteria. It was critical that all teams had to work together for overall success. For example, the director in charge of the Accounts Payable system had to be concerned about the work being done by her counterpart in charge of the

General Ledger system. To foster an environment of cooperation between the directors, I worked with senior management to implement some shared incentives, i.e., bonuses based on the overall success of the project, and not just on any one individual's or group's accomplishment. It's amazing the way people work together when they know that they'll only get a reward if the entire project succeeds.

Even if your company fosters a culture that creates boundaries and an environment that rewards individualism over teamwork, a good manager can shatter those behaviors. If you expect your team to work closely, it's best to set the example by working closely with your own peers.

"A good leader takes a little more than his share of the blame, a little less than his share of the credit."
Arnold H. Glasow, humorist

CHAPTER 8
If You Can't Stand the Heat, Get Out of the Position

When I was fairly new to a company, I walked past an executive office and saw one of my direct reports inside with an uneasy look on his face. I innocently poked my head in the doorway and quickly realized that he was being admonished for calling a meeting with this VP's staff without informing the VP beforehand. Once I understood the BS situation, I innocently said, "Oh sorry, that was my fault; I should have included you on the prior email chain." The reprimand immediately ended and I remember what my direct report said as we walked back to my office: "I can't believe you just did that for me." This one small encounter created a bond between us that has continued to this day.

I witnessed an extraordinary act of leadership while working in the banking sector. After being directed to immediately implement a risky change by a manager from another department, one of my coworkers made what he thought was an insignificant modification to the online computer systems during working hours. Minutes later, we learned that the consumer banking screens across the country had crashed. When we finally figured out what was wrong, the change was quickly reversed and the systems were brought back online. My boss was calm but extremely firm as she admonished my friend for what he had done. But what happened next is something I'll never forget.

A few hours later our team was summoned to a conference room where the director of the bank's online business department was waiting. Before we even had a chance to sit, he immediately began a scathing tirade of the importance of the online computer systems. When he was finished, he wanted to know the name of the individual who made the change, while never mentioning the person from his staff who had requested the modification. As I stared straight ahead, not wanting to give any indication as to who was guilty, my boss politely sidestepped the question, instead assuring this irate man that the person in question had already been reprimanded. Unrelenting, the exec continued to ask for the person's name over and over again. Finally, my boss replied with a measure of aggravation, "You want the name?" The man nodded fiercely and readied his pen to write it down. My boss slowly spelled out her own name and announced that she was the one who was ultimately responsible. Incredible, right?

Here's how this example of leadership manifested itself in my career several years later: We had just completed the conversion of a payroll system. Everything seemed fine until the first production run. As soon as the paychecks were delivered, my phone started ringing. To my surprise and horror, the checks were incorrect. And to make matters worse, this run happened to include the incorrect paychecks of executives who were paid once a month! Bad luck all around. It wasn't long before I was called into the CEO's office. When he questioned me about the specifics of what went wrong, I quickly assured him that we had already found the problem, fixed it, and were taking steps to ensure it would never happen again. Relieved yet determined, he continued pressing me for a more in-depth explanation of the problem. Not willing to incriminate the subordinate who caused the glitch, I replied solemnly, "It was my fault; I forgot to move a control file into the production environment." This savvy CEO was no fool; he knew exactly what I was doing. He smiled and said sarcastically, "I didn't know directors were still doing programming tasks." I just nodded and left his office. After that encounter, I think he respected me more.

It's important that you stand up for your team. Give them the benefit of the doubt and show them that you are on their side; this is the only way to create the bond required for success. At the end of the day, as a manager the buck stops with you; you're ultimately responsible when things go wrong. If you're willing to throw your staff and teammates under the bus, they'll be very willing to return the favor.

"If you want to control someone,
all you have to do is to make them feel afraid."
Paulo Coelho, novelist

CHAPTER 9

You Seem Somewhat Familiar; Have I
Threatened You Before?

Insecurity is the silent killer of any organization. And
here's the proof: It was my first week at a new job. The
day was rainy so the lunchroom was packed. I grabbed
a quick sandwich to go, anxious to get back to my desk
and read some more system documentation while I ate.
As I was paying the cashier, I glanced up and noticed
my new boss and his boss, the C, sitting at a nearby
table. I quickly lowered my gaze and tried to sneak by,
but cringed when I heard my name being called. My
boss was motioning to me to join them to eat lunch so I
reluctantly complied. What happened next was not only
bizarre, it was unimaginable.

A well-dressed man made his way up to the cashier.
While paying, he looked toward the C at my table and

asked politely if he'd had a chance to follow up on something. I watched in shock as the man sitting across from me, one of this company's highest leaders, immediately narrowed his eyes, clenched his jaw, stuck out his middle finger and blared, "Screw [and I'm using the nice word here] you! Since when do I work for you?" All heads turned and the crammed lunchroom went silent. The mortified man lowered his head and mumbled an apology before quickly walking out. I was horrified.

When our uncomfortable and awkward lunch finally ended, I followed my boss into his office and closed the door. I wanted to discuss what had just happened and get his take on it; was it really acceptable behavior in this company to be humiliated by this DICKtator? I respected my boss but wanted to make sure he knew that I could never handle being treated like that. No job was worth that amount of degradation. My boss readily agreed since he had witnessed the antics of this tyrant far too often and had found that the best way to battle him was to ignore him. Fortunately, he was high enough on the food chain to do just that.

No surprise that this toxic C's behavior actually created a culture of insecurity. It was rampant throughout his entire organization. No one gave an honest opinion if it wasn't considered to be good news or popular. Ideas were discussed and reviewed, over and over, scrubbed of every possible element that might enrage this guy. You know, analysis paralysis. Everyone was afraid to take the initiative lest it not be sanctioned by this maniac. He ruled by intimidation, not leadership, and as a result, the organization withered under his control.

After a major disaster recovery test of our computer systems to ensure we could run our business from an off-site location in the event of a catastrophe, we presented our findings to the C's in the board room. The test was not a complete success because one of the key components couldn't be properly replicated off-site. The CEO was visibly disappointed and firmly directed that the system be fixed and re-tested immediately. When I walked out of the room with one of my peers, she broke down in tears. I was shocked at the emotion and didn't understand where it was coming from. I led her into a nearby conference room to talk. Maybe something had happened in her personal life?

80

When she was finally able to compose herself, she explained that she was upset at what the CEO had said. What? I couldn't believe what I was hearing. Then I realized that she was a product of the reign of terror from the same C in the lunchroom story. She'd been mistreated by him for years and now was so worried that this one system glitch, along with the disappointed words from the CEO, would destroy her career.

Another unfortunate result of working for this terrorizing C was that many of his direct reports had inadvertently inherited this toxic management style and thus brutalized their own teams. I guess in their battered minds they figured that he was an example of how management must act. So not only had this C made life miserable for his direct reports, his style of intimidation trickled down to all the unfortunate underlings below within his span of control.

I haven't worked with this C in many years, but whenever I get together with friends from that company, his name is always brought up in a negative light. Only a BS manager would want this type of legacy.

Fear of reprisal breeds insecure employees who are afraid to make decisions. And this behavior doesn't only manifest itself at the lower levels of an organization. Here's an example of how it also exists at the top: In an attempt to give a few members of my senior team exposure to upper management, I began inviting them to the system reviews requested by one of our company presidents and his team. He was seeking to develop a new global management reporting system that would be fed from the data warehouse to help identify future sales opportunities. We worked hard on the design to ensure that all of his business requirements were met. Everyone left the initial meeting with action items, and follow-up dates were set. In every subsequent meeting, this president failed to complete his assignments. He continually waffled on important decisions. I eventually had to stop inviting my managers to the meetings; it was too embarrassing. So what happened to the project? It faded away and was never completed. John C. Maxwell said, *"Inability to make decisions is one of the principal reasons executives fail. Deficiency in decision-making ranks much higher than lack of specific knowledge or technical know-how as an indicator of leadership failure."* We all know that sometimes decisions are difficult because there are so many paths to go down and the correct choice isn't always obvious; the truth is that sometimes you have to make a decision, then make it the right decision.

Let's look at a non-corporate example. What I particularly enjoy about viewing sports is the interaction professional coaches have with their players. I watched with great interest when the 1994 New York Rangers hockey team went on to win their first Stanley Cup in over 54 years. Their coach, Mike Keenan fascinated me. Known as "Iron Mike," he was reported to be a taskmaster and strict disciplinarian. He was intimidating and consequently despised by many of his players. His coaching record was erratic, being fired or resigning from many NHL positions. The Bleacher Report, a well-respected sports media company, includes him on their list of the *10 Most Hated NHL Coaches of All Time*. I know what you're thinking, *"But he won the Stanley Cup!"* Yes he did, but why was he replaced after only one season? Especially in light of the New York Ranger's big victory? It's an interesting story for sure. In contrast, let's take a quick look at another NY hockey coach.

The Ranger's biggest rival has always been the cross-town Islanders. Since I am an avid Rangers fan, I've done my share of booing this other NY hockey team. But their record while Al Arbour was their head coach is hard to ignore. Under Arbour's tutelage, the team found almost instant success by attaining fourteen straight playoff berths, starting with their third season. They went on to win four consecutive Stanley Cup championships with him and are recognized as one of the great dynasties in NHL history. Their nineteen playoff series wins under Arbour remains unmatched in professional sports.

But more importantly, Bob McKenzie from The Sports Network characterized the Islander's eight-time Stanley Cup winning coach this way: *"He was always patient and caring and friendly with inquisitors and for a young media guy breaking into the business that was appreciated more than he would ever know. Arbour and his boss, Islander general manager Bill Torrey, were great at their jobs. At their very core, though, you could tell they were just good people. Al's players loved him. Over the years, when I would work in TV with former Islanders, first Glenn Healy and now Ray*

Ferraro, they would always speak so lovingly of him. They had great insights into him as a coach and wonderful, funny stories of him as a man, which made him all the more endearing. Their respect, admiration and affection for him came off them in waves."

So there's no doubt that despite opposing styles, both of these men were successful coaches. But there's one big difference: whereas Keenan was able to win the championship once, Arbour's team won it many times. Keenan's tenure with the Rangers lasted for only one season. His inability to connect with his players and management led to his departure. On the other hand, Arbour not only led the Islanders as their head coach, but he subsequently worked for the team in an executive management position. In dramatic contrast to Keenan, Al Arbour is ranked in the Top 50 on the Bleacher Report's list of *Top Coaches of All Time*, and not just the NHL, but in all sports.

An intimidating, insecure, micromanaging style may be effective in the short run, but it's obviously not a viable strategy for long-term success. Connecting with your team on a personal level is vital for repetitive achievement. Don't get the impression that "nice" means being a pushover or a consensual leader. I challenged my teams as much as anyone, but it was always done in a respectful way. Author Simon Sinek sums it up this way, *"If you want to be a great leader, remember to treat all people with respect at all times. For one, because you never know when you'll need their help. And two, because it's a sign you respect people, which all great leaders do."*

Being direct doesn't mean that you have to be disrespectful. And being nice doesn't mean you shouldn't be direct. If you initiate a conversation with an attitude, most likely the person you're addressing will respond the same way. One intimidating manager creates a deadly snowball that has no choice but to roll down the mountain and sweep up everyone in its path. Theodore Roosevelt once said, *"People ask the difference between a leader and a boss. The leader leads, and the boss drives."*

"The day firing becomes easy
is the day to fire yourself."
Tom Peters, author

CHAPTER 10
The Worst Part of the Job

I had been in a new job for only about two weeks when I received a call from my boss summoning me to his office. He pointed to his conference table and asked me to sit. I immediately sensed something was wrong because he seemed more formal than usual. I silently reminded myself that I hadn't yet been at this job long enough to screw something up; I couldn't imagine what was on his mind.

Straight to the point, he informed me that I had to fire one of my direct reports. What? I was shocked; I barely knew that poor guy. When I asked why, he replied, "Because he's a malcontent; he just left my office and was already complaining about you. He thinks he should have gotten your job and he's pissed. He's got a big ego, one that's not supported by his performance.

He's probably never going to fully support you, so you might as well fix the problem right now."

You can imagine how I felt. I didn't want to fire anyone, let alone this guy. I hadn't even had a chance to evaluate his abilities for myself. It just didn't seem right. I spent a sleepless night thinking about what to do. The next morning, I convinced my boss to let me take away some of the guy's managerial responsibilities instead of blatantly firing him. He reluctantly agreed. Needless to say, even that was a tough message to deliver. Not surprisingly, he left the company on his own shortly after this demotion.

While in another job, I had an employee who constantly wanted to buck the system. He annoyingly questioned every minor task, and continually passed negative and unprofessional comments about the management team and his coworkers. He found fault with everything on a daily basis, including his direct supervisor. In an attempt to understand where all this animosity was coming from, I called him into my office numerous times, always wanting and willing to give him the benefit of the doubt. But our sessions could do nothing to make him happy. At one point I wondered if he was actually trying to get fired. After several attempts, always documenting a detailed "get well" plan that he didn't follow, I finally gave up and realized that I had no choice but to let him go.

After another restless night, I arrived at work early, thinking it only fair to tell him the bad news first thing in the morning. When we sat down in the conference room, I could tell that he knew what was coming. And he should have; I'd been clear in our previous meetings that if his performance didn't change, this would be the consequence.

As we sat there I began to think about all of the training he had received and the time spent in numerous counseling sessions with me and his manager. I personally had expended hours in an attempt to make him successful. I questioned myself as to why I hadn't been able to get through to him; I wondered if maybe I could have done more to turn him around. Then a sobering thought hit me: I'm not responsible for his being fired; he is.

90

This was just like the first story in this chapter where it wasn't my fault that the unsupportive manager was demoted; it was his choices that led to the demotion. Bottom line is that if you've done everything within reason to help someone succeed, including making sure they're in the right position (remember the peg and the holes?), then you've done your job. For me, this didn't make the conversation easy, but it helped. I wasn't accountable for a bad employee's actions. I finally realized that you can't fix everyone, especially if they don't want to be fixed.

In contrast to the stories above, an unfortunate reality within the corporate world is that sometimes people will need to be laid off due to no fault of their own. When I began getting involved in corporate acquisitions, it always bothered me that often times these mergers meant reductions in force, i.e., layoffs due to budget cuts or redundant positions. I tried to console myself that in many cases, if the company hadn't been acquired, they may have been on a going out of business path, at which time everyone would have lost their jobs anyway. The brutal corporate reality was that sometimes you had to cut off your finger to save your hand.

When I was in my forties, with the full support and encouragement of my bosses, I decided to go back to college to earn an MBA. Although this was a great opportunity and turned out to be a wonderful experience, the downside was that I had to agree to relinquish some of my responsibilities. The C's felt that the rigor of this program, including the extensive travel required as part of the international curriculum, necessitated that I reduce the number of my direct reports in order to focus on my education. After having burned myself out during the several prior years, I was actually looking forward to a break.

About a year later, the VPs at my level were informed that a major layoff was necessary. After studying the target numbers, I knew this reduction in force (RIF) would affect some long-term employees. Although my current team wasn't impacted, I wanted to be involved in the RIF process because some of the personnel who would potentially be terminated had worked for me in the past. We had a meeting where my peer VPs reviewed the RIF candidates one by one. I silently winced as each name was mentioned. Two very long-term employees (whose corporate demographics meant that their performance review ratings may have been changed to get them on the list) had recently started reporting to a manager that worked in another state. Worse, these employees had never even met their new boss in person, a ridiculous situation. I glanced around the table. I wanted to see if the fact that employees were going to be laid off over the phone, by a boss they didn't even know, bothered anyone else in the room. Obviously it didn't.

When unbelievably there were no objections, and the meeting started to adjourn, I stopped everyone and asked them to sit back down. I conveyed my concerns to the team, yet still no one objected. Stunned, I requested that I be the one to lay off these two veterans; it was the least I could do. When that sad day arrived and I gave these employees the dreadful news, both of them actually ended up thanking me for telling them instead of the boss they didn't even know; they appreciated my compassion and sincerity.

For most managers, terminations for cause, layoffs due to budget cuts, or demotions due to sub-par performance are the worst part of the job. Being a kind and empathetic manager doesn't mean you can escape making some of these difficult decisions. But regardless of the circumstances that precipitated the negative action, make it a point to always be respectful and considerate during these heart-wrenching conversations. After all, these are peoples' lives you're dealing with. When delivering this type of distressing news, always be clear and direct; you never want to give someone false hope. But you should always be nice. Please remember that being nice doesn't mean you don't have to make tough decisions. But being tough doesn't mean you shouldn't be compassionate.

*"Selecting the right person for the right job
is the largest part of coaching."*
Phil Crosby, author

CHAPTER 11
When Mr. Right is All Wrong

I worked with a very smart guy who was a visionary when it came to supply chain management. With his expertise, we developed the detailed design for an innovative new system. Then it was time to apprise the CEO. The first part of the meeting focused on the customers' requirements and the system's functionality. Our expert was able to explain in excruciating detail how the system would meet the users' needs, support the supply chain, and would enable the flow of information to all the downstream systems. Everything was going well until we started discussing the actual implementation and roll-out of the new system.

When the CEO asked our supply chain guru how many customers would purchase this system in the next six months, he unhesitatingly replied with an astronomical (and unreasonable) number, which was immediately documented. Next, the C asked for a yearly projection. Again and seemingly without any forethought, an unrealistic number popped out of his mouth. I was horrified! As the big boss began writing this number down, I felt that I had to intervene in order to save this man from himself. I looked at my loose-mouthed friend, pointed at the C and whispered, "He's writing all of this down. Be sure you're giving him numbers that you can achieve." The well-intentioned man thought for a second and immediately cut his over-exaggerated projections in half.

The take away is that this guru was a great asset when it came to a long-term vision and innovative ideas, but he was not the right person to project future sales. Eventually the day-to-day management and rollout of this system was given to another manager more skilled in that area. Our technical expert was Mr. Right in the design phase of this project and Mr. Wrong during the implementation phase. Some people are innovators and thinkers; some are get-it-done managers. It's critical to recognize someone's strengths (or weaknesses) and proceed accordingly.

During my time working on mergers and acquisitions, I met many CEO's who had been great at getting a business started and making it successful. But they didn't have the skill (or desire) to take it to the next level, say from $500 million in sales to $5 billion. Sometimes these were people with innovative ideas who happened to be in the right place at the right time and were able to experience success as the business took off. But they weren't prepared for their company's future growth.

I have to admit that although I was a good computer programmer, I wasn't a great one. What I lacked in natural ability, I made up for by working extra hard. Over the years, I advanced and was eventually promoted into my first management position; this is where I was able to utilize my more natural ability as a coach. So while I was a decent individual contributor, my real value to the company was my ability to lead teams effectively.

I watched with interest the career of a really great programmer from another department as he began his ascent up to the management ranks. This man hadn't been just smart when it came to computer systems and business processes; he was brilliant. After he'd been a manager for a few months, I began receiving invitations to lunch from people who were working for him. These were good workers who I'd known for years and none of them were happy. It turns out that their new boss never gave up his old position in his own mind when he accepted the management slot. He wanted to do both jobs, and insisted on being involved in every phone call, even those due to system problems in the middle of the night; he didn't know how to let go of the details. He persisted in making all the decisions for the team and worked unthinkable hours, expecting the same from his staff. He was a controlling manager who overpowered and suppressed his team. He refused to give his subordinates the responsibilities that would help them grow. Several people from his group were so frustrated that they requested to be transferred. After a few months of his around-the-clock work ethic, this new manager had dark circles under his eyes and looked like a zombie. His promotion was not only a detriment to his health, but to the entire department. He wasn't a leader; he was a doer.

Corporate BS

When I contrast my career with this brilliant technician, I have to admit that he was a far better programmer and I was a better manager. Sometimes it's important to recognize that when someone isn't performing in their current role, their ultimate fit may be at either a lower, (or dare I say) a higher position within the organization. Imagine that! This concept is counter to what we are all trained to think, i.e., advancement based on a traditional path of jobs leading from the bottom up in the corporate job hierarchy. But as illustrated above, this may not be the best way to utilize a person's innate strengths and skills.

Here's an interesting tidbit: Wayne Gretzky is frequently recognized as one of the best hockey players of all time, and yet he was a losing coach. He couldn't make the transition into coaching and failed when forced to focus on the big picture, the entire team. In contrast, Mark Cuban got fired from his salesman job at a computer store before starting a consulting business which transformed him into a millionaire. Now a billionaire, he's widely regarded as one of the most successful entrepreneurs of all time.

Prior success doesn't always guarantee future success, and failure in one position doesn't mean a person won't be competent in another one – even if it's at a higher level. When selecting members to build a team, the evaluation of personnel must extend beyond the fact that a person was effective at a different level in the past. It's critical to evaluate the specific skills of the role that they were successful in and carefully compare them to the skills required for the new position.

"Consensus is the absence of leadership"
Margaret Thatcher,
Former UK Prime Minister

CHAPTER 12
From Great to BS...Another One Bites The Dust

Watching a great company transform into a BS one is heartbreaking. We've all heard of the book, *Good to Great;* maybe someone should write one titled, *Great to BS.* I've had the unfortunate experience of witnessing this type of corporate metamorphosis on a few occasions.

The Good.

I had just accepted a new job and was instantly thrust into the middle of an in-process and behind-schedule Human Resources system conversion. After reviewing the project plan, I immediately began calling daily morning meetings so I could review the critical path tasks with the team, get status updates, and make adjustments in resource allocations if necessary. During my second meeting, I questioned why one of the attendees hadn't completed the simple assignment that in yesterday's meeting he had promised would be done. He immediately apologized and assured me that he'd take care of it right away. I thanked him and moved on.

Afterward one of my new direct reports came into my office, shut the door, and explained to me that the person I'd just questioned about finishing a menial project plan task was the Executive VP of Human Resources. An hour later, the exec called me to let me know he had completed the assignment. I was amazed that during the entire project, he never once mentioned his title nor used it as an excuse for not pulling his weight on the team.

Weeks later, when I was at the company's orientation meeting for new employees, that same HR exec was in the front of the room and asked an intriguing series of questions: "How many of you have a doctorate degree?" A few raised their hands. "How many have a master's degree?" More hands. "Bachelor's degree? Associate's Degree?" When finished, he looked at the hundreds of new excited employees and stated bluntly,

"I want you to know that at this company, degrees don't matter, but performance does!" I knew right then I was not in a BS company. This was a place where I would have a chance to thrive based on what I could do, not what was on my résumé. For the next several years I was privileged to work with an amazing team of executives. They were all smart, challenging and fair. This was a great company. Unfortunately, things changed.

The Bad.

As time went by, many of the top executives began retiring. Who could blame them? They had completely dedicated themselves to the company, often at great personal cost. Now that they were getting older, I assume they felt it was time to start new chapters in their lives. The resignations happened in quick succession, like the domino effect: first one, then one more, then another. Soon almost all the C's were replaced. A new team was hired and I immediately started to notice vast differences.

The new CEO, as well as a few other C's, were brought in from companies outside of our industry; with them came a new corporate culture. Top leadership demanded that, with the aid of highly paid outside business consultants, we all develop utopian "Mission Statements." Each subsidiary had to have one, along with every department within. Now instead of business plans, we were directed to develop obscure goals and write "Vision Statements." The previous leadership's non-BS, "get it done" paradigm was being replaced by what lower level managers called "All BS, All the Time." As if that weren't bad enough, we were then directed to create team "slogans." There was even a contest where every slogan was hung on the "Holiday Christmas Tree" with an award given to the best one. Needless to say, mine didn't win the contest.

Another obvious change centered around those pesky items called "details"; they were no longer required. At executive status meetings, I was never asked a challenging question; I just had to show up. No one expected you to know details, and if you did, you were criticized and told you needed to operate at a higher level.

Then I observed an interesting phenomenon: What do leaders who have no real knowledge of the business, nor a desire to learn details, actually do? They do reorganizations! (Or what I call the merit badge of the BS manager.) Clearly, some reorganizing can be a good thing and is necessary for a company to thrive. But when they're executed without thorough analysis and consideration for the impact on sales, customers, and support teams, it becomes obvious that it's being done because it's the only way for a BS manager to feel like they've accomplished something. It's wrong.

As if things couldn't degrade any further, we now found ourselves entangled in an inordinate increase in the number of meetings. Although it seemed like all I did was attend meetings, nothing was actually getting done. About this time I was asked to help out with our teams in Asia. No problem; I welcomed the challenge. However, then I found out that management wanted me to be an "observer" and report back, i.e., I had no authority to make necessary changes or hold anyone accountable. I was traveling halfway around the world to attend meetings with no significant outcome. And I wasn't the only one. But as long as we were traveling, my boss was happy because he was able to report to the CEO that he was providing worldwide support.

So this new executive team brought us slogans, mission and vision statements, fewer details, reorgs, more meetings, and international travel for no reason. But what came next was even worse.

The Downright Ugly

Our corporate culture had changed so much that I felt like there should have been a new category added to the Employee Performance Review form: politics. The mantra instilled by the prior regime that you were judged based solely on performance was now replaced by a bunch of people who were talking their way onto the field.

Rather than surrounding themselves with people who could be depended upon to tell them the truth, the new C's were more interested in who would tell them exactly what they wanted to hear. About this time many of the best VP's and managers throughout the organization began resigning. They weren't willing to accept this new BS culture. One of my friends and colleagues summed it up nicely, "This new regime transformed my career into a job."

But it got even worse. The C's decided to institute something they termed "Shared Leadership." Basically this meant that no one was allowed to be in charge. I can't tell you how much time, money and effort was spent on this new corporate-wide initiative which turned out to be pure BS.

I was asked to attend a meeting to come up with yet another slogan. This one was going to be printed on coffee mugs which would be distributed throughout our department — whoopee! I was reminded that even though I was a VP, because of the Shared Leadership initiative, I was to attend the meeting as a "consultant." I was instructed to only contribute to the process or interject my thoughts if I was specifically asked for help. So I sat in the back of the conference room and watched as ten great people went to work. They connected a laptop to a projector and the debate ensued. Everyone was trying hard to come up with something catchy, but soon they were talking over each other as chaos replaced order. With no one to take charge, the meeting ended hours later with no slogan. This BS continued for three consecutive mornings, finally producing a phrase so catchy that I can't even remember it.

The great leader Margaret Thatcher sums it up quite nicely: *"Ah consensus ... the process of abandoning all beliefs, principles, values and policies in search of something in which no one believes, but to which no one objects; the process of avoiding the very issues that have to be solved, merely because you cannot get agreement on the way ahead. What great cause would have been fought and won under the banner 'I stand for consensus'?"*

Another product of our Shared Leadership initiative was increased management training, usually not a bad thing. A meeting was scheduled with fifty or so supervisors and I was to be in attendance. Again, I wasn't supposed to speak unless specifically asked for my opinion. Workbooks were distributed detailing example after example of extraordinary leaders doing great things. Attendees read about Mahatma Gandhi, Nelson Mandela, Martin Luther King Jr, Abraham

Lincoln and Winston Churchill. Then the team was asked to complete self-evaluations to determine if they had what it took to be a great leader. I remember one well-intentioned manager raising his hand and asking me, "How will I know when I'm being a leader?" I explained that sometimes a particular situation provides the opportunity to demonstrate great leadership skills. For example, before the 9/11 terrorist attack, New York's Mayor Rudy Giuliani was widely recognized as an exceedingly good manager. However, the horrific events of that day propelled him into the national spotlight. And his decision making during the aftermath of this tragedy revealed (and tested) his true leadership skills. If it weren't for that catastrophic event, no one outside of New York would have paid him much attention, and he certainly wouldn't have had best-selling success with a book titled "Leadership." I didn't want to say it, but we had created an environment where the desire to create consensus through Shared Leadership eliminated any chance of demonstrating true leadership skills.

Perhaps you can relate to this next indication that the company was moving into the downright ugly. I agree with the old saying "No one plans to fail, they simply fail to plan." But with this new set of executives, all we did was plan. We were infiltrated with six sigma "black belts" and actually had plans to track planning, yet nothing was getting done. Remember, this was a company that had done multibillion-dollar integrations in a matter of months. In this new environment, we couldn't develop the plans for the plan in that time frame! Process had taken the place of human intelligence.

After a few months under the new regime, I found myself sitting in one of the business sector president's staff meetings. Each of her direct reports from the sales organizations were asked to present their plans for the following quarter. The new CFO was in attendance. After everyone was finished presenting, the president and new CFO informed them that their sales goals weren't good enough; they were too low. They were instructed to go back to their teams and increase their projections. Their sales goals were obviously being set from the top down, not bottom up; already a recipe for failure. But wait, it gets even more interesting.

The next week we were back in the same conference room, and the same senior sales members were presenting their revised numbers. One by one they went through their new plans. Then one highly respected executive stood and displayed his numbers on the screen. I referred back to the sheets from the prior week and noticed immediately that they hadn't changed. Everyone assumed that he had pulled up the wrong file. When the brave exec was questioned by the CFO about the numbers, he replied, "The numbers are the same because before I presented them last week, I had already challenged my team to be aggressive, yet realistic. If you ask me for the numbers again next week, they'll be the same. And if you want me to just make up unrealistic sales projections, then someone else can do this job, because I won't." The room went silent. Someone courageously suggested that we take a break.

Years later, when many of the new BS C's were gone, this defiant executive was promoted to one of the top positions in the company. He was so effective that even after he eventually retired, they asked him return to help when another executive was let go.

Sometimes we fall in love with the companies at which we work – and often, love is blind. If you see your beloved company going from Great to BS, follow the lesson in Chapter 1.

"Each person holds so much power within themselves that needs to be let out. Sometimes they just need a little nudge, a little direction, a little support, a little coaching, and the greatest things can happen."
Pete Carroll, NFL coach

CHAPTER 13
The Best Part of the Job

During my first week of my earliest computer programming job, I made what I thought was an insignificant change to an online file. Minutes later, my phone rang; it was from an internal number. I wondered who in the world it could possibly be calling me since I didn't know anyone else at the company. A man I had never met quickly introduced himself as a manager and informed me that the file I had just modified (incorrectly) was used by hundreds of computer programs. People from every company office were now getting errors because of me. Yikes! To his credit, he delivered the catastrophic news calmly but directly. Flustered, I apologized profusely and explained that it was my first week at work. I was surprised that he didn't just throw me off the phone and rush to fix the error himself being that so many people were impacted. Instead, he patiently coached me through the steps required to repair what I had done, thereby ensuring that I would never forget how to do it. His kindhearted guidance created a bond between us; from that point on, I never hesitated to call him for advice. This experience taught me firsthand that a manager also has a role as coach. Every leader has the opportunity to impact someone's life and help them become better.

Here's another coaching story that had a pivotal impact on me: The first time that I was assigned to lead a major project with implications far beyond my traditional responsibilities, my boss wisely appointed a more experienced individual to act as my coach. This woman was exceedingly smart and had been responsible for many similar assignments in the past. Initially I wasn't thrilled about being shadowed since I assumed it indicated a lack of confidence on my boss' part. Grateful for the opportunity to manage a large team on a critical program, I quickly got over my own ego and was determined to show the company what I could do.

As weeks passed and the project progressed, my coach unobtrusively observed from the sidelines. I remember being in a large meeting where someone pointed to my "shadow" and asked a question about the overall strategy. She quickly replied in a respectful but firm tone, "I'm not the one running this project." She never attempted to take over and never did anything to give the impression that I wasn't in charge. I have to give her a lot of credit that despite being tremendously more experienced than me, she never tried to persuade me to do things exactly as she had in the past. In fact, she supported me when I seized the opportunity to streamline existing processes and procedures. Nevertheless, she took her role as coach very seriously and sincerely wanted to help me learn and grow; whenever she saw an issue that I should be aware of, she would meet with me in private to discuss her concerns, careful to never coach me in public. In retrospect, my "shadow" was immensely helpful, taught me a lot about humility, watched my back, and shined light on potential problems without drawing attention to herself. How fortunate I was to have such a wonderful leader as a coach. The experience with her really resonated with me and I vowed someday to be able to do the same for someone else as I progressed up the management ladder. And here's how I finally had the opportunity to do just that.

I had a great employee who was an outstanding and ambitious computer programmer, but it became obvious that she wanted to transition into management. She certainly worked harder than most and had demonstrated all of the skills to succeed. The only problem was that like many people, she had an extremely difficult time with public speaking. When she confided this to me, I immediately wanted to help. I began inviting her to meetings that had nothing to do with the specific projects she was working on just so I could ask her a question that she'd have to answer in front of a crowd. Over the next year, she became more and more comfortable speaking in public. Eventually, it was time for her first big presentation. I purposely left her name off the agenda of the meeting just in case she got the jitters at the last minute. When it was finally her turn to speak, I saw the fear in her eyes; she looked at me, her eyes wide in horror, and inconspicuously shook her head. I quickly gave her a reassuring smile, stood and did the presentation myself. No one in that room ever knew that she had panicked.

After the meeting, she rushed into my office and broke down in tears. I assured her that it was fine; we would give it a shot in another meeting. I told her that I didn't care if we had to repeat that scene one hundred times; we were in this together! The next opportunity she had to give a presentation, she was awesome! I consider this one of my best accomplishments. When she was promoted to a management position, I don't know who was more proud. This employee went on to have a wonderful career, and each time she advanced, I felt a great sense of satisfaction. The most rewarding aspect of my job was when I had the opportunity to help others succeed.

And lastly, here's a quick story of how even a few minutes of a manager's time can make all the difference. While I was preparing a critical presentation for a very large audience, the CEO took the initiative to seek me out while I was practicing in the auditorium. He provided not only encouragement, but important hints on the best way to utilize a teleprompter, something I had never done before. He explained the nuances of reading off of multiple screens to ensure I was making eye contact with the entire audience to keep them engaged. He also suggested that I tailor the speech (i.e. sentence length and cadence) to coincide with the natural rhythm of my voice so that I wouldn't run out of breath. I can't begin to tell you how many times I've thought about his brief, yet thoughtful coaching session which made all the difference.

Everyone's career goes through bumps and bruises; believe me, I've had more than my share. When we're in a slump, we need extra attention, training, coaching, compassion and understanding. And we need to be willing to give these things to others when they're struggling. Taking the time to help teammates succeed is a critical characteristic of the non-BS manager. Be willing to coach and to be coached.

*"It is not titles that honor men,
but men that honor titles."*
Niccolò Machiavelli, historian

CHAPTER 14
*Badges? We Don't Need No Stinkin'
Badges!*

As I begin to write this chapter, I can already sense my
blood pressure rising myself as I relive the following
past events. What started out as my best and most
rewarding year in the corporate world turned out to be
my most difficult. I was assigned the lead position on a
massive multibillion-dollar company acquisition and
system integration project. This was my dream; the
largest, most complex and aggressive conversion our
company had ever done. I was confident because I
knew we had the team in place that could pull it off –
no doubt!

Because of the criticality of this project and challenging
timeline, my life immediately changed. I went from
flying commercial to taking corporate jets; from
meetings with team members, to meetings with the

auditors who would approve the sale; from being a topic on the board room meeting agenda to being the agenda. Imagine my surprise when I found a handwritten note on my desk one afternoon from the CEO asking for permission to visit one of the new branch locations. He was asking me for permission! This was a really big deal.

As the conversion progressed, I was tasked with a tough assignment: I had to give a presentation to over 600 members of management from the combined companies. The prospect of speaking in front of so many important people made me more nervous than the conversion itself! My goal would be to explain the overall conversion process, instill confidence, and make them excited to see the value in the new tools and systems that their teams would have access to…all despite the fact that their company was just bought-out. I knew that there was a lot riding on the success of this presentation; it was critical because we needed to get buy-in from each of the purchased company's management team. Without their support and enthusiasm, the conversion would surely be a disaster. I took this task very seriously and devoted many hours to develop the content and to polish it. I not only wanted it to be informative, but eye-catching and compelling as well. With much valuable input from all of the team leaders on the project, and with the help of our slick marketing and graphics experts, we created a kickass presentation that included inspiring imbedded videos. Hollywood couldn't have done a better job!

After flying out to California along with the CEO, I was anxious to make my presentation. When it was finally my turn to be on stage, my mentor gave me an incredible introduction and I confidently – at least on the outside – walked up to the podium. The spotlight was on me as the lights dimmed and the show began. I went through the pitch, acknowledging the struggles and sacrifices the teams would endure to get their divisions converted. I explained everything from the intricate timeline, to the amazing new tools being developed specifically for their teams. Because of the lights, I couldn't see much of the audience, and was somewhat taken aback on how complete silence filled the huge auditorium; you could have heard a pin drop. It was very dramatic. When I finally finished and the lights came back on, I bit my lip as I waited for the reaction. I wasn't sure if I had succeeded or failed. But my fears were unfounded as I immediately received a standing ovation! I attempted to introduce the next speaker, but couldn't quiet the crowd. This was incredible! All my hard work had paid off and I felt like I had achieved a huge accomplishment for our company. I left the stage and walked into the hallway to get some water for my cotton-dry mouth and was immediately accosted by our CEO who slapped me on the back and said effusively, "I can't believe what you just did!" To hear these words from someone I respected so much was overwhelming. I know what you're thinking: this doesn't sound like failure. But just wait...

Shortly after an extremely successful conversion, our CIO left to "spend more time with his family." Since I believed that I had more than proved myself by leading many large projects, including that huge integration described above, I assumed that I'd be a shoe-in for the vacant CIO position. Not only did I believe I deserved it, I wanted it, and wanted it bad. After expressing my aspiration to senior executives, they agreed to consider me for the position. But there was one catch: I had to go through the same interview process that all of the other candidates from outside our company would be subjected to.

My first meeting was with a representative from the world-renowned executive search firm that had been retained to fill the open CIO slot. I had to drive to LaGuardia airport to be interviewed in the Admiral's Club. It was a bizarre meeting. Expecting to be grilled on my professional experience and accomplishments, I was surprised when the questions started with ones about my background prior to my career. They began with my childhood and eventually focused on my high school days. The interviewer blurted out a series of rapid-fire questions about the clubs I belonged to, sports I played, and whether or not I was a class president. I became frustrated because I didn't understand why, as the only internal candidate with a lengthy proven and verifiable track record, I was being treated like a complete stranger.

Several weeks later, I was informed that I didn't get the job. Needless to say, I was upset, very disappointed and disillusioned. To make matters even worse, my failure to get the job now had to play itself out in front of my peers and subordinates, all who knew that I was being considered. I was well-liked and well-respected, and because of my standing ovation-worthy speech, along with many successful company conversions, my teammates had been confident that the job was mine. They were shocked when I was rejected. I tried not to outwardly react to their disappointment, but inside I was certainly hurting.

I decided there was only one way to deal with this situation. But, surprise, it had nothing to do with quitting. I realized that I had been blessed to be working with the best and most talented people on some of the most exciting projects of my career. I wasn't going to let not having a title take that away. Even though I wanted to crawl under my desk and hide, I held my head high, went back to work and did my job. In retrospect, not getting that position turned out to be a blessing. I had been lured by the title, but now I can admit that in reality, I had been more fulfilled running large challenging projects than I ever would've been in that C position.

By the way, a few years later, the new CIO who got the job also left "to spend more time with his family." Bottom line, titles aren't everything. Sometimes it's all about the work.

"Employers and business leaders need people who can think for themselves - who can take initiative and be the solution to problems."
Stephen Covey, author

CHAPTER 15
You Get What You Give

We've all heard it said that initiative is the key to success. Too trite to be true? Not so fast. Remember my first job in the defense industry? After being there for just a few months, one of the lead software engineers abruptly gave his notice. Everyone was shocked. The team of about twenty-five people were called into a conference room and asked a question: "Who wants to take over his work?" Initially no one raised their hand, and for good reason: he had been responsible for an extremely complex system that managed the wiring diagrams and engineering drawings that were used during the construction of Navy fighter jets.

You probably already know what's coming next. When no one volunteered, I gathered my courage and raised my hand. The entire team knew I was a rookie, so they burst into laughter. Embarrassed, I immediately looked down and silently admonished myself for what I'd just done. Luckily the supervisor surprised the roomful of people by thanking me; and then he unbelievably added that I'd be considered for the position! I was eventually awarded the job, and with help from my boss, I learned, maintained and enhanced that complex system until I left the company.

This single act of courage (or maybe what seemed like stupidity at the time) became a pivotal point in my career. Once I proved to myself that I was capable of maintaining and enhancing these intricate programs, it gave me the confidence to tackle bigger challenges. This increased my visibility throughout the organization and eventually led to me quitting my first job to begin that successful consulting career.

Here's another story: The firm I worked for acquired a new company and my team was called upon to convert a small portion of their computer systems. We subsequently completed the project successfully, on time and within budget. A few weeks later, I was in my boss's office to discuss my next task. I casually mentioned that one day I'd like to have the opportunity to run a full merger team, not just one facet of it. I'll never forget what happened next: he gasped in astonishment and a piece of the sandwich he was eating flew out of his mouth and across the desk. It was obvious that he thought I was nuts! After all, who was this young inexperienced idiot to be asking for such a large responsibility? I didn't say anything, but when I walked out, I was determined to prove him wrong.

Through a lot of initiative, hard work, desire and determination (along with great subordinates), I was able to be successful on my subsequent projects. I ended up not only holding this position multiple times, but I held it during the largest and fastest integration in the history of electronics distribution. Having courage paid off.

One of the main reasons I was able to transition from being the "IT guy" into other areas of the business was because I always wanted to know the big picture. I not only wanted to understand the business logic behind the specific part of the project for which I was responsible, but also the areas of the business that came before and after it, i.e., the entire lifecycle. That's what I found fascinating. I thrived on being able to gain business process knowledge so I could help identify areas that could benefit from system changes or new technologies. I wanted to effect change for the company, not just one department. It was this constant desire and initiative to learn the business that ultimately resulted in me being assigned to projects and teams that encompassed more than my technology background.

One more example comes to mind: At one point during my consulting career I was assigned to work a job at a prominent Wall Street investment bank in downtown Manhattan. On my first day at work, I drove my car to the train station, took the hour-long trip to Brooklyn, and then was pushed (literally!) onto a subway car so crammed with people that I felt like an unwilling participant in a public orgy. After a ride under the East River, I walked several blocks and eventually made my way into the lobby of a gigantic skyscraper. After enduring a ride in an overcrowded elevator, I exited onto the eighteenth floor. I showed the guard my ID and passed through the door. I was surprised at what I found: hundreds of people sitting at crammed desks with no walls or partitions to hide them. I eventually found my boss and was ushered to an abandoned spot.

A few weeks later, my group was assigned to work over a long holiday weekend in order to implement a new large computer system. Although as the new guy I didn't have any particular tasks to perform during this install, I decided to take the arduous trip into the city anyway as a show of support. Once there, I quietly figured out a way I could help and spent hours at a corner desk painstakingly cross-checking reports to online screen images. My boss eventually noticed and questioned why I had come in, especially since I wasn't getting paid. I was honest and told him that I just wanted to help the team. He nodded his head and thanked me. However he obviously never forgot that day since after the company went through a major layoff, I was one of the few remaining consultants still working at the company.

So is initiative critical to success? You bet. Bobby Unser, the great race car driver, said, *"Desire! That's the one secret of every man's career. Not education. Not being born with hidden talents. Desire."*

*"Management needs to get out of the office
and out and about to communicate
with the people of the organization."*
Tom Peters and Robert H. Waterman, authors

CHAPTER 16
*What We Have Here is a Failure to
Communicate*

As previously mentioned, one of my bosses when I worked in the travel sector was an office hermit. We rarely ever saw her. Once and awhile we'd get a glimpse when she would skulk through the hallway, head down, and disappear into the ladies room. When she needed to provide a live update to the team, it was obvious that she was miserable. How a person who didn't want to talk to anyone could be given the responsibility of supervision was a mystery to me.

I've worked with many executives who demonstrated endless amounts of energy by waking early and going to the gym, but who wouldn't expend the calories to leave their office to ask a question of someone who sat ten feet away. As we all acknowledge, face-to-face communication has been challenged by the technological advances of email, instant messaging and texting. But personal communication is vital to maintaining the health, satisfaction, and motivation of the team.

I had an acquaintance who worked as a senior executive for a major bank; he had a really big job with lots of responsibility. Unfortunately he was laid off. When he called and asked me to help him find another position, I immediately agreed and told him to send me his résumé. The document arrived attached to a blank email, i.e., no message, no text. As the weeks went by and our online communications increased, I realized something disturbing: it was all about him. He never asked how I was doing and never typed "thank you." Not once did he personalize his message in any way. Often the only words in his online correspondence were in the subject line. It didn't take me long to recognize why he was having trouble finding a job. He didn't know how to establish a friendly, genial rapport with anyone (and probably didn't care to waste time doing so). How could he ever build the professional relationships he would need to succeed if it appeared that he was just a people user? The individuals you work with need to know that you're interested in them. That's the only way they'll return the favor.

I know what you're thinking: as a manager, you can't be close friends with your staff. To which I say, BS! Although there's a fine line between friendship and being someone's boss, as long as the relationship is built on honesty, and doesn't compromise your actions, it not only can co-exist, but it can thrive.

When a long-term employee that I had never met was assigned to work for me, it turned out that both of his sons were good friends of mine from a previous job at another company; we even used to work out together at a local gym. I was a bit concerned about having their father as a subordinate, wondering if it would sour my friendship with his sons. Let's face it, anything I did to piss off this employee would certainly be communicated back to his boys. I was especially apprehensive whenever it was his Employee Performance Review time. Every year this was challenging because my seasoned employee would continually remind me in advance that his review was approaching, and I knew that invariably, we'd have the same debate: he wanted to be promoted to a manager, but I thought he was better off in his current position as an incredibly valuable technician. Each time, our annual discussion started with some tension, but I was always determined that it not end the same way. After I pointed out that his natural abilities made him excel as a technician, not a manager, and backed this up with examples, he would end up agreeing before leaving my office. I had been able to make him see that I truly had his best interests in mind and wasn't trying to hold back his career.

One of the most memorable days during my career was when I attended the wake for the mother of a director who worked for me. Unfortunately we were in the middle of a huge project, so I couldn't attend the afternoon service. By the time I left work it was dark, cold and snowing...and late. I pulled up to the funeral home and rushed inside. Because of the weather, most people had already left; only a few family members remained. When the employee saw me rush into the room where his mother's body lay, he broke down in tears. But what he did next is what lingers in my mind to this day: he rushed up and hugged me fiercely, saying, "I knew you would come." Then he repeated, "I knew you would come." That was the best compliment I could've ever received. I still get teary-eyed just thinking about it. Real managers show up for their people. Relationships are everything.

I learned an important lesson from my wonderful mentor: something she called, "R before I"…"relationship before issue." She had just been promoted to a C position within our company as the only female at the executive level. To help with the transition, she was assigned a personal coach. He taught her the "relationship before issue" rule and it's something I always try to follow both in and out of the office. How can you work with people on a daily basis, trying to solve complex problems under great stress, if you don't have the solid foundation of a relationship with them? I put in the effort to get to know the people I worked with and make sure they knew that I cared about them; because I did.

For most parents, conversations about their children are welcome and uplifting. Imagine how good it would feel if one of your bosses actually knew your kids' names and hobbies. Unfortunately, when the tone of communication from boss to subordinate is cold and formal, one can be sure that the response will be the same.

I always strive to be considerate while communicating in both my personal and professional life. If one of my teammates is having a bad day, and I have an issue to discuss with them that could wait until tomorrow, I wait. When I have to discuss a difficult situation with my mother, I postpone the conversation until I can talk to her in person. With electronic communication there's no chance to observe facial expression or voice tone. How many times have you received an email that seemed harsh (i.e., written with what you thought was a "mean voice"), only to find out the harshness was not intended? I admit this has happened to me many times.

Non-verbal communication also plays an important role in establishing relationships. Here's a story: During my first really big assignment with an aggressive deadline, I had an idea that I hoped would garner buy-in from the team. As soon as everyone was notified of their involvement on the project, I called a kick-off meeting to review the objectives and timelines. When the session ended, I stood at the doorway along with my managers, and we shook each person's hand as they walked out of the conference room. This had a very positive effect on the team: it was a non-verbal sign that we were all in this together and we appreciated their help; the handshake signified our mutual commitment to the task at hand. Looking someone in the eye while providing a firm handshake shows the respect you have for the other person and how you value their participation. And I think my teammates got the message.

As work progressed on this project, our group was so tight that the guys on the team took a cue from the sports world and decided that during the final stretch they'd quit shaving. Sounds really dumb, but I have to tell you, not only was it fun, but it served to bond the team together. Unfortunately, I have the most scraggly and unattractive beard in the history of mankind, so while walking through the hallways and passing a teammate, they would often start laughing. We held "ugly shirt" days and did all kinds of other crazy stuff while never losing sight of critical priorities. After a few of these types of projects were completed, people who had never volunteered to be on one of these large teams were actually asking to be included.

It's a no-brainer that if you don't like to communicate, you shouldn't be in management. One of the C's that I reported to actually called me into his office one day and pleaded, "I need your help; I can't motivate the staff. I'm the type of person that you put into a room for a few hours with a bunch of spreadsheets and I'll come out with an answer. But I'm no good at inspiring a team." So you have to wonder why in the world he took a job that included having to motivate people.

Most studies show that the number one reason people leave jobs is not for money; they leave because they don't feel appreciated by their management. How can anyone feel valued if they're not communicated with? If you show you care, it will come back to you tenfold.

*"Accountability is the glue that
ties commitment to the result."*
Bob Proctor, author

CHAPTER 17
Houston, We Have a Problem

It's a well-known fact that our government squanders
enormous amounts of money — from over $46 billion
in canceled defense projects to the National Science
Foundation's unbelievable $3 million expenditure to
study shrimp on a treadmill. Although we may find it
hard to comprehend this degree of mismanagement in
government, I've witnessed my share of reckless and
unaccountable spending in the corporate world as well.

It was extremely frustrating when the initiators of large
corporate investments were never held financially
responsible for sponsoring projects that didn't live up to
the hype. Rarely was the promised return on
investment, which provided the "compelling case" to
initiate the project, ever revisited once the
implementation was complete. Many times resources
were allocated to someone's pet project because it was

going to benefit the company in ways us non-visionaries couldn't even begin to imagine. *Really*?

But most companies I worked for were negligent in measuring the financial success of these dreamers' expenditures; it was almost as if once the money was spent, it was water under the bridge — so why waste time going back to analyze it? I would hazard a guess that it was because they were afraid to know the results. Without being held accountable, the same managers continued time and time again to advocate for additional BS work. We kept putting the same players on the field without measuring results – sound familiar?

Case in point: After a new, exceedingly smart CEO was hired, he insisted that we implement processes to measure profitability at a detailed level. Soon we were putting systems in place to quantify Return on Working Capital (ROWC) for each of our customers. This calculation provided the discipline to ensure that the lifetime expense (i.e., how quick the customer pays, field support required, age of inventory, etc.) was compared to actual profits. Things certainly got interesting when the reports were produced. One showed that for many years, despite enormous sales to one of our premier customers, we had been making little to no profit. This was not just any customer; it was a hundred-billion-dollar-plus corporation with international brand recognition. Everyone was shocked. After reviewing the data for accuracy, we eventually realized that the cost of providing field support and specific systems required to service this high-priority company was staggering, and resulted in ridiculously low returns.

These reports initiated serious conversations on whether we should be terminating our relationships with highly recognizable, brand name, yet unprofitable, customers. When a team of executives presented these customers with undisputable data, they eventually agreed to pay a fair price for the services they were receiving. You get the point. And it was all because a savvy CEO understood the importance of measurement and accountability.

Not all squandered or misappropriated corporate profits are related to high-profile projects or customers. Sometimes executives spend company profits like drunken sailors. Early in my career, I was working at a job where my cubicle was located directly across from an empty office. Once the new C was hired, I had a ringside seat to the absurdity that transpired. He and the facilities manager spent hours in meetings to discuss his new furniture and wallpaper. No BS! Over the next few months I watched as his office was first painted, then wallpapered, and then wallpapered again. Of course, the first set of furniture wasn't good enough, so another had to be ordered. Was this really the best utilization of this C's time and company resources? Who was holding him accountable? Was he so insecure that it was all about "the show?" How could he act this way in light of the fact that he was being observed by the rank and file?

Meanwhile, one the most respected CEO's I ever worked with had no problem working in a grossly understated office with outdated furniture. He was apparently secure enough to know that it wasn't about appearances; obviously he cared about whether or not he was squandering the company's money. Which one of these C's would you rather have running your company?

I remember watching a Bill Moyers interview with historian Thomas Frank. During their interaction, Moyers asked, *"What happened to the moral compass?"* To which Frank replied, *"It was demagnetized by money."* Make sure you don't get demagnetized.

"Growth demands a temporary surrender of security. It may mean giving up familiar but limiting patterns, safe but unrewarding work, values no longer believed in..."
John C. Maxwell, author

CHAPTER 18
Your Get Up and Go has Got Up and Gone

You may have seen a chart similar to the one below mapped to the lifecycle of a business from inception to dissolution. However, comparable characteristics of behavior can be linked to our own careers.

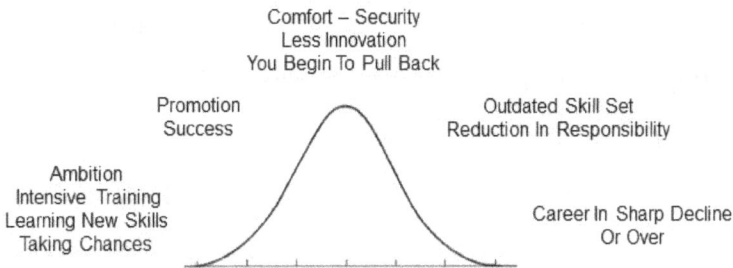

Comfort – Security
Less Innovation
You Begin To Pull Back

Promotion
Success

Outdated Skill Set
Reduction In Responsibility

Ambition
Intensive Training
Learning New Skills
Taking Chances

Career In Sharp Decline
Or Over

Your Career Lifecycle

We all begin our careers with lots of energy. We have drive and determination to increase our skill set. We enjoy establishing business relationships, often seeking out other energetic, up-and-coming workers like ourselves. At this stage, we're not averse to taking risks. This amount of career vitality and focus frequently leads to promotions. And once we've been rewarded with increasingly advanced positions, we understandably feel successful and proud of ourselves. As we should! We're secure and competent in our jobs.

But unfortunately after this point, we sometimes become complacent. It was certainly true in the beginning of my own career that once I was comfortable in a position and felt I was doing a great job, it was much harder to drive myself. When I achieved more success than I'd ever expected, or even felt I deserved, I have to admit that I often fell into the trap of basking in that success. My motivation diminished and complacency began taking its place. I recall languishing in this slump for about a year before becoming reenergized by the challenge of a managerial promotion. For the second half of my career, which was comprised of various management positions, I found that just having the opportunity to mold and develop teams was the only incentive I needed. I enjoyed waking up and going to work each morning, and relished the challenges that the day would bring.

In your role as the CEO of your career, the objective is to stay on the left side of this chart. You should climb and ascend the Bell curve many times as you learn new aspects of your current job or move into new positions. Some of you may plead the excuse of being too old (you know, "You can't teach an old dog new tricks"). It may be true that you don't want to, but don't blame it on being old. Age has nothing to do with your ability to learn new things and stay motivated. But your attitude certainly does.

Ten US presidents were inaugurated when they were in their 60s. Ronald Reagan, who many consider a great leader, was almost 70 when he was inducted. Donald Trump was 70 when he was elected. Only two presidents were under 45: Theodore Roosevelt (42) and John F. Kennedy (43). The vast majority of presidents have been over 50 when they occupied the White House. In recent years, most of the top presidential candidates have been in their late 60s or older (i.e.,

Hillary Clinton, Mitt Romney, Joe Biden, Donald Trump, and Bernie Sanders). So age is not a factor.

During my career, I never heard anyone mention that someone was "too old" to function in their current position as the rationale for letting them go. I did hear many times that their performance was subpar, that their skill set was outdated, or that they had no passion for work.

Before you slide down the right side of the curve due to inattentive momentum, decide what you want your future to look like. Admittedly, retiring can be a worthy and admirable goal. But so can another position within your current career. Or maybe even a new career altogether. Years before my desire to remain in the corporate world diminished, I became passionate about writing. I finally took the leap and found myself energized and excited about transcribing all the words in my head onto a page; it still gives me a thrill. Maybe you want to open a restaurant or become a teacher. Whatever it is, you can do it!

Corporate BS

"I've missed more than 9,000 shots in my career. I've lost almost 300 games. 26 times, I've been trusted to take the game winning shot and missed. I've failed over and over and over again in my life. And that is why I succeed."
Michael Jordan, basketball great

CHAPTER 19
Don't Stop Believing

As mentioned above, during my years doing merger and acquisition work, I had the opportunity to visit C-level executive offices across the country. I noticed that many of these leaders had the same poster hanging on their office walls, the list of the trials and failures that Abraham Lincoln had endured on his way to being one of the greatest presidents of all time. Check these out:

- 1816: His family was forced out of their home and he had to work to support them
- 1818: His mother died
- 1831: Failed in business
- 1832: Ran for state legislature – lost
- 1832: Lost his job; wanted to go to law school, but couldn't get in
- 1833: Borrowed money from a friend to begin a business and by the end of the year he was bankrupt. He spent the next 17 years of his life paying off this debt

- 1834: Ran for state legislature again – won
- 1835: Was engaged to be married, but his sweetheart died and his heart was broken.
- 1836: Had a total nervous breakdown and was in bed for six months
- 1838: Sought to become speaker of the state legislature – defeated
- 1840: Sought to become elector – defeated
- 1843: Ran for Congress – lost
- 1846: Ran for Congress again; this time he won. Went to Washington and did a good job
- 1848: Ran for re-election to Congress – lost
- 1849 Sought the job of land officer in his home state – rejected
- 1854: Ran for Senate of the United States – lost
- 1856: Sought the Vice-Presidential nomination at his party's national convention – got less than 100 votes
- 1858: Ran for U.S. Senate again – again he lost
- 1860: Elected president of the United States

What if Lincoln was judged only by his early career? What if his many failures made him give up? Would you and I have kept going in light of these disappointments?

While attending school, I worked as a bartender. This was a fun job and it paid incredibly well. But I knew it wouldn't be my career. While goofing around at home with an old portable computer, I became intrigued.

I wrote a few simple programs and found myself becoming more and more fascinated. One night after the bar closed and I was cleaning up, the owner walked in. We sat down and had an early morning beer together. He was a very successful, self-made businessman. As we sipped, he inquired about my future career plans. When I confided my new-found curiosity about computers, he was very encouraging. More than that, he was happy to hear that my long-term goals had nothing to do with his bar.

A few days later, he called to tell me that he'd spoken to an acquaintance of his who was a computer project manager and arranged for the man to meet with me. Interested to find out what a real programmer did for a living, I was excited to go.

The project manager was waiting for me in his office. For the next hour, he did nothing but try to discourage me from this occupation! He was a bit gruff as he described all of the bad aspects of the profession. He couldn't emphasize enough that he had a horrible job. I was surprised; this is not what I had expected. I wondered if he had an ulterior motive or if he was just one of those negative people with a chip on his shoulder. I remember driving home questioning if I should just keep working at the bar; the pay was good and, as mentioned above, I was having fun. I continued tinkering with the computer in my off time, writing simple programs as amusement. After a few more weeks, I made the decision that I was going to follow my dream, despite what the cranky, malcontent guy had told me.

The next step was to find a good school. Luckily, there was one that had a two-year course in programming not too far from my house. In a stroke of good luck, I found out that the next semester was just about to start and there was still availability. Everything was looking good and I just had to pass a logic test before I could be accepted. I figured no big deal, so I confidently took the test.

A week later I received my grade and was shocked. Not only did I fail the test, I had failed it miserably! Every page of my completed exam was covered with red ink. Wow, what a bummer. I had approached my new venture with a measure of confidence, but now I was left second-guessing what to do. Was I really not cut out to be a programmer? Needless to say, my drive home wasn't pleasant. Unsure, I continued working at the bar for a few more weeks before finally deciding that I wasn't going to give up. It took me a while to get the courage to call the school again and ask if I could retake the test. The sympathetic administrator said that even though it was against policy, he wouldn't report the results from my first test and would give me one more chance. But he warned me that I better study hard if I wanted to pass. *Yes*! Fortunately, my bar job afforded me the luxury of having free time during the day, so for the next few weeks I spent countless hours in the library, reading and practicing with every logic test I could find. Then I took the entrance exam again.

I can remember going to back to get my test results as if it were yesterday; there was so much at stake. I walked into the administrative area and the kind manager motioned me into his office. His face showed no emotion as he opened a folder and handed me the results. The first thing I noticed was the lack of red ink. When I looked up, he was smiling. My score was one of the best he'd seen. Not bragging, but it darn well should have been based on how much time I had spent preparing! And, I had to take it twice!

My trip home this time was certainly different. I was accepted into the school and spent the next two years working very hard to excel. I even graduated with good grades. When I think back, I realize that if I would have given up, either because of the discouraging project manager, or the failed first test, I might still be tending bar and missing the incredible experiences my corporate career presented.

Marilyn vos Savant said it artfully, *"Being defeated is often a temporary condition. Giving up is what makes it permanent."* And she wasn't kidding!

One of my biggest challenges growing up was reading. I always was and I still am a very slow reader. Even though our family didn't have much money, I was blessed to live in a town with a great school district. After taking several tests in grade school, it was determined that I had dyslexia. Another result of this diagnosis is that I'm also a terrible speller. Not a great combination for someone who writes books! But I certainly didn't let this hold me back. I truly believe that my early struggles in life built my "never give up" attitude. Non-BS people don't give up!

"Strive to become the type of employee you want to work with, the type of manager you want to work for, and the type of leader that you admire most; when you've done this, you've achieved true success."
A.D. Napier, author

That's a Wrap!

As you now know with certainty, this is not a book by some Ivy League academic (I wish!) filled with elaborate concepts and theories. It's just the reflections of an ordinary guy with real-life corporate experience. Whether you sit in an office or in a cubicle, hopefully you've found that some of my BS stories resonated with you. Reflecting on my business career has been a wonderful experience; I only wish I could go back and fix so many of the mistakes I made along the way. But maybe my words can help you avoid some of my pitfalls.

Success in business, and more importantly in life, can be measured by the amount of meaningful, long-lasting relationships we've cultivated; something that money can't buy. I truly believe that these connections helped me achieve career goals that I never thought possible.

And most importantly, have left me with enduring friendships I treasure to this day.

Stay in touch with colleagues, not because you need something from them, but because you value their friendship. Every year around my birthday I still receive a card with a handwritten note from my mentor even though we haven't worked together in years. It's a piece of mail I always look forward to receiving.

The most satisfying times of my career have been when I've had the opportunity to help others succeed. As mentioned in the previous chapters, for me this was always the best part of the job. Do yourself a favor, take a look around your organization and identify one good person, a really hard worker, and make it part of your job to encourage them, to help them, to mentor them. Believe me, the rewards you reap will be more than you can imagine.

Remember to always shoot for the top. If a bartender with dyslexia, with blue collar expectations, from a lower middle-class family, who happens to be a terrible reader, and an even worse speller, can go on to write books, just imagine how much more you can achieve.

Jack Ducey is quoted as saying, *"The biggest obstacles in our lives are the barriers our mind creates."* Never limit yourself; you will have enough people in your life trying to do that for you.

Leaders are people who challenge the status quo, look for more efficient ways of doing things, and are willing to make tough decisions. But true leaders gladly stand on the sidelines while others get credit. A leader is not someone who attends meetings, takes notes and does exactly what they're told. That's a doer, not a leader. And sometimes we show leadership by letting others lead. We take the role of manning the label printer so others can accomplish critical tasks.

If you happen to run a company, shepherd your people and make dreams come true. As a leader, you've been given the wonderful opportunity to impact so many lives. Renowned strategist Michael Porter said, *"Good leaders need a positive agenda, not just an agenda of dealing with crisis."* Be uplifting, challenge your employees respectfully, and be sure to take good care of them.

Be passionate about your job and career. If you can't, it may be time to find another one. If your position is making you miserable, it's probably reflecting in every other aspect of your life. Try to be honest with yourself; constantly evaluate your career, not only by how much money you're making, but by how much satisfaction you derive from it. Be the person that other people smile at and are genuinely happy to see walking in their direction. Be fair and when you have to be tough, be compassionate.

I would be remiss if I didn't take time to thank everyone who helped me in my corporate career. I'm not going to document specific names because the list would go on for many pages. From the great teams I had the pleasure of working with, to my peers who kept me sharp, to my bosses who pushed me to higher levels than I ever expected to achieve — I can never thank you enough and I couldn't have done it without you.

I'd also like to thank you, the reader, for taking the time to read my BS book. I hope you've found it worthwhile. To continue the conversation, please visit our online community at www.CorpBull.com. Here, you can join our BS newsletter, nominate one of your great bosses to the *"Best of the Best List,"* or recommend new items for inclusion on our *"You know you're working for BS management if..."* list. Hope to see you there!

www.ingramcontent.com/pod-product-compliance
Lightning Source LLC
Chambersburg PA
CBHW032001190326
41520CB00007B/312